HOW
YOU CAN
PROFIT
FROM
GOLD

HOW YOU CAN PROFIT FROM GOLD

James E. Sinclair
& Harry D. Schultz

Arlington House
333 Post Road West, Westport, Connecticut 06880

How You Can Profit From Gold is an updated and revised
edition of *How The Experts Buy and Sell Gold Bullion, Gold
Stocks and Gold Coins* published by Arlington House Pub-
lishers, 1975.

Library of Congress Cataloging in Publication Data

Sinclair, James E
  How you can profit from gold.

  Edition for 1975 published under title: How the experts buy
and sell gold bullion, gold stocks & gold coins.
  Includes index.
  1. Gold. 2. Investments. 3. Hedging (Finance) I. Schultz,
Harry D., joint author. II. Title
HG293.S54   1979   332.63   79-27278
ISBN 0-87000-473-5

Manufactured in the United States of America

Dedicated to the hopeful expectation that
man will rediscover the principles of
fraternity in the days ahead.

Contents

8 Contents

Introduction

A Devil's Advocate on Gold

THE SUBJECT OF gold tends to introduce passion and dispute into the calmest of economic discussions. Gold has little intrinsic value, yet men have launched fleets, sacrificed lives, and squandered fortunes in its quest. The Bullionists, followers of a 16th and 17th century school of philosophy, held that the accumulation of gold was the proper central purpose of a nation, and that success in this drive would translate into power and prosperity for a people.

Few today would accept the Bullionist view, yet half a century after most of the world's major trading nations formally abandoned the gold standard, the pricing and distribution of gold is a matter of major concern to statesmen, economists, bankers, and many investors. Efforts to demonetize gold—to remove it as a factor in the creation of currencies—have largely failed because no other medium of exchange offers the discipline of gold. We are stuck with the metal. So let's examine what is wrong with gold.

One obvious flaw is that as a medium of exchange, it is very heavy and cumbersome. You can't put a million dollars' worth of gold in your pocket; it weighs something like 200 pounds (down from a ton only a few short years ago), and it takes up a lot of room. You can, however, put a million dollars' worth of shares, or a letter of credit, or a checkbook in your pocket.

Pure gold is too soft to be used as coinage; it would bend and literally wear away. Perhaps that would be the ultimate in inflation—where we all had 100 percent pure gold coins and nothing else, and they just got smaller and smaller through wear till the gold supplies of the world disappeared. You HAVE to mix gold with other metals to be able to use it in any real sense. While gold bars are made of nearly pure gold, people don't and can't hand those around for their weekly groceries, or even for car purchases.

Gold thus has little practical use in bulk. Yes, it is used for some types of glass windows to preserve heat, it is used for certain areas of space travel and for electronics, but these are fringe uses. Its main function is to be looked at. We hang it on ourselves, stand it in our homes, or hide it in vaults and tell ourselves it represents wealth when we look at it.

But we don't and can't really use it.

It is also very expensive to produce. One must process an enormous amount of rock, dug in the most horrendous underground conditions, to extract this yellow metal, ounce by ounce. And for what? For a metal whose biggest use is to be looked at?

People rob for it, people die for it. Governments overthrow whole institutions for it. Henry VIII dissolved the monasteries in England and claimed he had a new religion, partly because he wanted to take a new wife, but mainly because the country needed wealth. With the monasteries dissolved, their gold holdings and priceless altar vessels and ornaments could go into the government treasury.

Isn't it all rather startling as the world moves into the 1980s —with complex computers, instant communications, and massive data at hand on almost every subject under the sun—that in such a seemingly advanced world a man's word cannot be sufficient backing for his international trading?

How much time and energy are spent, pain and misery are caused, because man is still barbaric. He must use a silent, nearly useless master, a metal, as a way of forcing himself to keep his word when trading with others.

But won't gold become outdated? Surely at this stage of civilization we can look into the very near future and see that something less barbaric than gold can govern our international trading. But what is there to choose? NATO? The UN? The International Monetary Fund has proved it can't do the job. At this point in time it would seem that no man or body of men is capable of controlling money honestly and fairly to ensure its international stability.

Man just isn't honest. It is a terrible admission, but he isn't. Governments have brought the Western world to the brink of economic disaster, where many of us live in fear of losing everything we have. Prices of goods and services have increased a hundredfold in a period when the amount a single man could produce has also increased a hundredfold. The equation here just doesn't come out right. When a man can produce ten times more per man-hour than he could, say, fifty years ago, prices should be much less than they were fifty years ago—this would be logical. But governments stepped in. They meddled with money. Yet we sit back and praise the politicians who say, "You have never had it so good, look what we have done for you."

What they should say is, "You have never had it so good. Look how the intelligent among you, the inventors and entrepreneurs, have raised your standards, and even we in government, with all the grandiose plans that we made you pay for, couldn't take away all the effects of honest-to-goodness inventive progress."

And so we come back to gold. Not because we believe in gold. Gold is more a devil than a God. Gold is a monument to man's barbarity, not to his highest self. It is a reminder that without some sort of mutual economic weapon that everyone can use, man's inhumanity to man, man's greed, man's lust for power and fame will cause him to lie, cheat, steal, distort, and—if he is a politician—to do so with a smiling face, saying it is for your own good and in the public interest.

Gold is a weapon as primitive as the bow and arrow. To date nobody has invented economic gunpowder, although perhaps one day somebody will. Like atomic energy, suddenly a new concept of energy, *economic* energy, will break forth and start a new era. The splitting of the atom launched us technologically into the space age, but the rest of the departments of our life haven't caught up with that. Emotionally, economically, and in our relations to one another we are still in the stone age, and until we can break into the space age in these areas, we are stuck with a stone-age medium of exchange.

Look at the munitions business. Society has always looked down on these "merchants of death," as they have so often been labeled. People get emotional about it from time to time. Remember the antagonism toward the Krupp works? How students have demonstrated outside the factories of Du Pont and similar manufacturers of war material? But the munitions business is booming, if you'll pardon such a low pun.

Munitions sales continue to expand, even in the most economically backward areas of the globe. Mass murder continues to occur. Killing for religious motives has not disappeared, as we have seen in Iran. Does this mean that guns and bombs themselves are to blame? Or should we rather put the blame on the real villain, man himself? Man simply hasn't evolved far enough yet to do without guns, wars, and killings.

And just as we can't blame guns for man's barbarism, neither can we blame gold.

Around the Persian Gulf and in the Middle East, man has recently taken recourse to barbarism as a means of settling differences of religion and political opinion. Not very advanced, is it? Neither was Vietnam.

Man has not perfected any techniques for getting along with his fellow man. Or woman. Divorce rates hit new records every year. Crimes of violence are also increasing. Small wonder, if we don't understand our own psychology and know almost nothing of the human brain, that we need a monetary system based on something tangible. In gold we trust. In words we mistrust. And, so far, rightly so.

Man *may* evolve enough in time to escape this dependency. But, in my opinion, it will take a thousand years.

And *until* man has evolved, maybe we should be grateful that we have gold, for it will always work; it can help pull us out of a hole. In a world where we send men off to be killed in the name of patriotism or in the name of somebody else's government, in a world where wars are still being fought because of clashing religious views, in such a world gold doesn't look so terribly barbaric.

It's strange that the politicians who resent the controlling mechanism of gold despairingly refer to gold as a barbaric metal. It is not that they are condemning gold as much as they are pretending that man is elevated above barbarism. He isn't, not really. And until he is, then I must reiterate that, much as we may dislike gold for symbolizing our lack of evolution, gold is going to be around—to scorn us silently when we try to remove it from our monetary system. Gold will be there when, out of chaos and misery, we put our monetary systems back together again. Gold *is.*

We needn't like it, but it is—and I am a realist, not an idealist.

If I may be permitted to offer my vision of the world in 1985 and speculate on what happened to gold, I think the scene would be something like this:

Gold coins had been issued by most countries and were actually in circulation (they started to appear in the early 1980s, even though the money system had come under extreme pressure earlier). Money became so suspect by the 1980s and paper currency rates became so erratic that governments were inclined to mint gold coins to reestablish confidence in money. They found out they could legislate what was legal tender but not what was money. Central banks began accumulating more gold, buying on the free market, and some bought directly from South Africa. The Middle East nations had built up gold reserves far above any previous levels, through an ambitious purchasing program easily financed by their oil sales to the rest of the world.

When the International Monetary Fund was forced in the early 1980s to use gold as the de facto cornerstone of the world system, inflation popped like a hot balloon. Prices dropped. This caused some unemployment and business slowed down, but stability returned and money again became something you could save without fear that it would rapidly lose much of its value. There were exchange controls in effect in the United States. That distorted everything, and official U.S. rates and world rates on currencies were vastly different.

All of the professors who grew up bottle-fed on Keynesianism had been repudiated. A new respectability had returned to gold and gold shareholders since the period we can barely remember during the late 1940s, 1950s, and early 1960s when gold was considered something going out of style in this very advanced world.

Actually, man wasn't as civilized as he thought. If the premise is valid that man has not evolved enough to push gold aside and substitute fiat money, then clearly one is correct in moving into gold investments. If we are correct in holding that gold's continued ascendancy will escalate sharply in the 1980s, it is still incorrect to be 100 percent in gold. My recommendation is to posture one's portfolio to be at least 50 percent in various forms of gold investments. This percentage should be increased over the next few years to 75 to 80 percent by 1985.

A portion of one's investment in gold should be, if possible, in gold bullion itself. This earns no yield and produces storage charges, but it is also free of mine flooding, mine fires, government mine taxes, stock confiscation, and so on. Another portion should be in gold shares, some of which should be high yielding, some low, for diversification. A small portion should be in gold coins, of common date variety—with minimum premium. Some people may fancy the gold futures market, too, but this is not for the majority.

The choice of gold shares should also produce diversification between South African shares and North American—mainly Canadian. A 75–25 split is recommended. As one approaches such a period of economic catharsis, all markets take on an air of volatility, including gold.

As I have pointed out many times, sound-money men tend to love gold because it gives discipline, thereby providing stability, a fair measurement, and freedom from inflation. But in fact we should perhaps say we hate gold, because man is so unevolved that gold is critically necessary to keep the beast in line.

Do you love the whip because it protects you, or do you hate it because it is still necessary?

Harry D. Schultz

Chapter 1

A Brief History of Gold

"The various necessities of life are easily carried about and hence men agreed to employ in their dealings with each other something which was intrinsically useful and easily applicable to the purposes of life."

—Aristotle

ECONOMICS TEXTBOOKS TRADITIONALLY cover the subject of money by explaining how mankind advanced from bartering salt, wampum, shells, and various other commodities as a means of exchange to trading more sophisticated forms of money. This leads into a discussion of gold, providing an opportunity to serve up all of the hackneyed descriptions and clichés regarding the metal as a "medium of exchange" and a "storehouse of value."

In textbooks, as well as in classroom discussions, the student is swiftly transported to Dullsville.

Yet anyone who makes even a cursory examination of gold's history will find that the metal has had a mystical appeal since the dawn of civilization.

Gold, it is alleged, came even before sex! Some scholars have observed that gold is mentioned in the twelfth verse of the second chapter of Genesis, before the creation of Eve.[1] God didn't make Eve out of Adam's rib until ten verses later.

But aside from this distinction there is no question that gold was one of the first—if not *the* first—metals to be known and used by man.

Croesus, King of Lydia (Western Turkey), is believed to have ordered the first gold coins to be struck in 550 B.C. Like the Pharaohs of ancient Egypt, the Romans, Greeks, Persians, Etruscans, Spaniards, and countless others, he had an insatiable desire for gold.

Man was not long in discovering that, of all the materials used as money over thousands of years, gold is the most nearly perfect money.

Why?

Gold is scarce, beautiful, indestructible, and extremely versatile. A single ounce can be beaten into a sheet covering one hundred square feet and an ounce can be drawn into fifty miles of thin wire. As David Ricardo pointed out, gold is not only an

[1]"And the gold of that land is good: there is bdellium and the onyx stone."

ideal measure of value but also is the *thing* valued. Its two uses, one as a monetary unit and the other as a commercial product, are often described as the "duality" of gold.

Whether it be in jewelry, dentistry, or electronics, gold has no peer in its usefulness. Year after year a relatively unchanging proportion—roughly 50 percent of the world's output of the metal—is absorbed by the arts and industry. Jewelry alone accounts for about one-fourth of the total annual use of gold in the non-Communist world.[2] Other industrial uses absorb a comparable percentage; the rest goes into private hoarding or investment, and official coinage use.

We find gold playing an important role throughout the course of history. The California gold rush of 1848–49 not only influenced the monetary history of the world; it also contributed to the metamorphosis of California from a remote and unsettled region to a bustling area. In the process, it caused San Francisco to grow from a village to a city in little more than a year instead of decades.

In Czarist Russia, too, gold acquired an important status in the economy that, incidentally, persists to this day, despite the fact that capitalist and communist worlds may be poles apart politically and philosophically.

Lenin once predicted that gold was only a temporary necessity and that after socialism triumphed over capitalism the yellow metal would be relegated to such functions as covering the floors of public lavatories. He turned out to be a poor prophet, just as misguided as the Keynesian economists who attacked gold as an outmoded metal destined for obscurity.

Not long after gold was discovered in Russia, a short-lived gold rush took place in Australia. Once again it produced a frenzied search by shoemakers, bakers, butchers, clerks, and all sorts of ordinary folk who joined in the hunt for quick riches.

The South African gold rush came years later. It proved to be a bit different from previous gold discoveries. In the vanguard of this boom were legendary figures like Cecil Rhodes, who already had struck it rich elsewhere. With some of his contemporaries, Rhodes had acquired a fortune in the diamond fields of South Africa. This, in turn, provided the capital needed to

[2]Most of the gold used in jewelry is 14-karat, in a scale of quality (purity) ranging from 1 to 24. Thus, 14-karat gold contains 14/24 gold or 58.35 percent.

undertake the costly development of the South African gold mines, which have since become by far the world's largest suppliers of the yellow metal.

Gold in Modern Times

John Maynard Keynes is one of those who dismissed gold as a "barbaric relic."

Actually, the worldwide acceptance and consistent demand for gold would justify the title "noblest of metals" in the twentieth century.

Until the outbreak of World War I, the monetary systems of the Western nations were closely linked to gold, and the gold standard performed relatively well.[3] But the war-induced outflow of gold from Europe so weakened the backing of European currencies that all of the major nations of the world, with the exception of the United States and Switzerland, abandoned the gold standard and suspended specie payments.

Leading economists of that era, including Lord Keynes of England and Gustav Cassel of Sweden, argued that "gold has failed, both as a means of payment and a standard of value." Subsequent American monetary legislation came to embrace this theory, based on the false premise that the gold standard was responsible for most of the economic ills from which the world suffered.

This theory of blaming gold for man's blunders has been effectively demolished by many competent authorities, including Madden and Nadler,[4] who, though by no means advocates of gold in all of its aspects, concluded that as a standard of value, as a basis for currency and credits, and as a medium of settling balances among economic political units, "experience has shown that no other metal can better perform this function and the complete abandonment of gold would lead to currency chaos."

[3]When economists refer to the "gold standard," they usually allude to not one, but several types of monetary systems linked to gold.

The gold bullion standard, for instance, obliged the central bank of a country to sell gold in stipulated quantities at a fixed price to meet international obligations.

The gold exchange standard called for the inclusion of foreign exchange as part of the legal reserve of the central banks on this standard.

The "limping gold standard," on the other hand, involved a percentage coverage of currency by a gold reserve backing.

[4]*International Money Markets,* Prentice-Hall, 1936.

Today, despite the U.S. Treasury's long attempts to downgrade gold as a monetary metal, the U.S. still holds one-fourth of the world's total gold stock, as against more than two-thirds in 1949. Germany is the Free World's second largest holder of gold with about 10 percent; Switzerland and France each have about 9 percent; Italy has about 7 percent, and the Netherlands about 5 percent.

United States Gold Policy

The United States, over the course of its history, has had shifting monetary standards. They have shifted so much that a look at the past is worthwhile, just as a matter of curiosity.

From 1862 to 1879 the nation was essentially on an irredeemable paper standard. U.S. notes (which came to be known as greenbacks) were issued in amounts far exceeding the nation's monetary requirements for that period. Since they weren't redeemable in gold on demand, naturally it was not long before they drove gold out of circulation—people kept their gold and did not spend or circulate it.

This was just one of many historical illustrations of Gresham's Law, which holds that bad money drives good money out of circulation.

Under the Coinage Act of 1792, a bimetallic standard had been established in which the U.S. dollar was defined as 24.75 grains of fine gold, or 371.25 grains of fine silver—a 15-to-1 ratio. An ounce of gold, therefore, was worth $19.42. But this ratio overvalued silver at the mint. Silver proceeded to drive gold out of circulation—only silver circulated for much of the period from 1792 to 1834, though the country ostensibly was on a bimetallic standard for that period.

An 1834 law reduced the pure gold weight of the dollar from 24.75 grains to 23.2 grains, and the price of an ounce of gold was raised to $20.67. Now gold was overvalued; this helped drive silver out of circulation.

In order to avoid an outflow of gold during the Civil War and thereafter, the nation went off the metallic standard in the 1862–1879 period. Paper currency no longer was redeemable in gold or silver.

In February 1873 the infamous "Crime of '73," as the antisilver legislation was called by the silver interests, was enacted; it dropped the silver dollar from the list of standard coins to be minted. The outcry led to the passage of the Bland-Allison Act in 1878, which required the Secretary of the Treasury to purchase silver to be added to the national monetary stock.

A True Gold Standard

In 1879 the nation returned to the redemption of greenbacks in gold. But a true gold standard wasn't instituted until the defeat of the silver interests, led by William Jennings Bryan, and the passage of the Gold Standard Act of 1900. This provided that the dollar, consisting of 28.5 grains of gold nine-tenths fine (23.22 grains fine gold), should be the standard unit of value. The nation was finally on a single gold standard with a statutory price of $20.67 an ounce.

Except for the 1917–1919 period when the disruptive effects of World War I compelled an embargo on gold exports (the embargo was lifted in 1919), the government's buying and selling price for gold remained $20.67.

Roosevelt Devalues

The Depression and the Gold Purchase Plan of 1933 brought about historic changes. On October 22, 1933, President Franklin D. Roosevelt said, in a historic radio address:

> Because of the conditions in this country and because of events beyond our control in other parts of the world, it becomes increasingly important to develop and apply further measures which may be necessary from time to time to control the gold value of our own dollar at home.
>
> Our dollar is now altogether too greatly influenced by the accidents of international trade, by the internal policies of other nations and by political disturbance in other continents.
>
> Therefore, the United States must take firmly in its own hands the control of the gold value of our dollar. This is necessary in order to prevent dollar disturbances from swinging us away from our ultimate goal—namely the continued recovery of our commodity prices.
>
> Therefore, under the clearly defined authority of existing law, I am authorizing the Reconstruction Finance Corporation to buy gold newly mined in the United States at prices to be determined from time to time after consultation with the Secretary of the Treasury and the President. Whenever necessary to the end in view, we shall also buy and sell gold in the world market.

Just three days later the official price of newly mined gold for that day was fixed at $31.36 an ounce. This was slightly above the world price.

Arthur M. Schlesinger, Jr., in *The Age of Roosevelt,* relates how Roosevelt, aided by Secretary of the Treasury Henry Morgenthau and Chairman Jesse Jones of the RFC, would fix the price of gold each morning while he ate his eggs and drank his coffee. Not infrequently they joked about "lucky numbers" and what the day's price would be.

Unfortunately the Rooseveltian blueprint didn't work. It soon dawned on FDR that his moves weren't having the tonic effect on the economy that he had hoped for. So, under the authority of the Gold Reserve Act of 1934, Roosevelt by proclamation on January 31, 1934, fixed the weight of the gold dollar at 13.71 grains of fine gold and the dollar price of gold at $35 an ounce, instead of the old price of $20.67. It was announced to the world that the United States would stand ready to buy and sell gold at $35 an ounce.

The Gold Reserve Act of 1934, unfortunately, not only raised the price of gold: it also prohibited the private ownership of gold. Only Americans using gold for industrial purposes were given licenses to obtain the metal, based on their proven needs.

The $35-per-ounce price prevailed from 1934 until 1971, when the official price was raised to $38 an ounce by President Nixon. Only fourteen months later Nixon again devalued the dollar, in February 1973, when the price of gold was raised to an official rate of $42.22 an ounce.

Implicit in the action was an admission that the U.S. Treasury's inflexible policy toward gold pricing had been a failure.

As Milton Gilbert, Economic Advisor of the Bank for International Settlements, has stated so eloquently: "The long resistance of the United States to a justified adjustment of its position by an adequate increase in the official dollar value of gold must certainly be the greatest self-imposed infliction in monetary history."

Chapter 2

Gold, Oil, and Inflation

"The prices vary much on the road and the eternal confusion with the good and bad money and its different value is enough to weary a bank clerk."
—*Diary of a traveler from London to Vienna in 1829*

ANY CURRENCY, REGARDLESS of the importance or strength of the country involved, requires reserve backing. Thousands of years of history have proved that as soon as a currency departs from its gold backing, that currency becomes a commodity—and commodities fluctuate according to supply and demand.

History also demonstrates time and again that an unbacked paper currency can only go down in value. That is what has happened in the United States. Since the 1930s, the money supply has tended to increase faster than the output of goods and services, creating built-in inflation that has reached double-digit proportions twice in the 1970s. Gold had once acted as a control over the amount of money outstanding.

Monetary expert Nicholas L. Deak has defined inflation in these simple terms: "Inflation occurs when a society is trying to do more than its resources permit. There is no such thing as controlled inflation. Rather you see creeping, walking, or runaway inflation. It builds up speed slowly, then goes faster and faster."

With the U.S. government constantly running budgetary deficits—that is, spending more than it takes in—more purchasing power has been put into the hands of the public than is withdrawn via taxation. Those continuing increases in the money supply have not been offset by gains in productivity and so people pay higher prices for a limited amount of goods offered for sale. Labor demands more wages to offset the higher prices, corporations raise prices to offset their higher costs, then labor comes back demanding still more, and the process goes on and on.

It is of course possible to blame part of today's runaway inflation on the soaring oil prices that have stunned the Free World since the 1973 Arab oil embargo. But the energy crisis has only worsened an already deteriorating situation. It is evident that politicians were caving in before the pressures of inflation in one country after another.

In the early 1970s, the Tory government in Great Britain—not the Labourites—increased the money supply at rates that approached 20 percent yearly. And in the United States, both Democrats and Republicans knuckled under to inflationary pressures.

Democrat Lyndon Johnson made little or no effort to finance the Vietnam War with a tax increase, contending that America could afford both guns and butter. By ruling out a politically unpalatable tax boost to finance the most unpopular war in U.S. history, he laid the foundation for a massive inflationary groundswell later on.

Republican Richard Nixon did little better. He, too, failed to come to grips with the economic problems facing the nation, much like his predecessor. Although he brought the Vietnam conflict to a conclusion, Nixon amassed huge budgetary deficits and, worse, introduced the inefficiency of wage and price controls, which only added fuel to the inflationary fires.

After Watergate washed Nixon out of office, his successor, Gerald Ford, displayed his zeal for combating inflation by producing a new slogan—WIN—for "Whip Inflation Now." That about sums up his program. The administrations of Presidents Ford and Carter continued to encourage more and more bank credit and monetary growth while maintaining a disdain for gold.

Is it any wonder, in the light of this record, that the United States has experienced a serious stock market reversal, the highest interest rates in the nation's history (because the Federal Reserve tried to do what the politicians refused to do), and the most severe erosion of public confidence since the Great Depression of the Thirties?

While this sorry economic record was being compiled, the U.S. Treasury's distaste for gold remained constant. In 1961 President Kennedy put an end to the right of U.S. citizens to own gold bullion overseas. President Johnson reduced and Nixon eliminated the 25 percent gold backing for Federal Reserve deposits. And President Nixon devalued the dollar twice within the short period of fourteen months.

The Impact of Oil

As the world faces inflation, recession, and unemployment, it also must deal with the incredibly complex problems created by a quantum leap in prices.

The monopoly power of a tiny handful of oil-producing nations gives them the ability to cripple the economies of the oil-importing nations, both developed and undeveloped. OPEC (Organization of Petroleum Exporting Countries) ran a current account surplus of $50 billion in 1979, and the International Monetary Fund (IMF) has estimated that the surplus will exceed $55 billion in 1980. Officially reported monetary reserves for the OPEC nations by mid-1979 had reached $44.6 billion, plus gold worth an additional $14 billion. These figures do not reflect the enormous sums represented by the private fortunes of individuals. In some of the oil-producing countries, it is difficult to distinguish between public and private accounts, a matter of considerable convenience to regimes that are not eager for the world to know the extent of their holdings or their investment decisions.

The reported reserves held by the OPEC nations increased fivefold from 1972 to 1979. This represented the greatest transfer of wealth in the world's history. The financial markets faced difficulties in absorbing the huge petrodollar revenues being accumulated by Arab and other oil-exporting countries. While a large proportion of the oil revenues formerly were invested almost automatically in U.S. Treasury securities, the inflation caused in large part by exorbitant oil price increases caused these securities to shrink in value. This in turn led the Arab money-managers to seek other forms of investment, notably gold. This shift in Arab investment strategy, which included dollar sales, has been one of the significant factors behind the decline of U.S. currency.

The SDRs Created

One of the unique inventions of the monetary experts has been the so-called "Special Drawing Rights" for gold (or SDRs) that were unveiled by International Monetary Fund officials in 1967. They were supposed to fulfill a role as a "new international reserve asset."

The SDRs were simply bookkeeping entries, created by the stroke of a pen. Each country was assigned a quota, based on its contribution to the IMF. The values the SDRs possessed resulted solely from the fact that members of the IMF assumed the central bank would accept them in settlement of their balances with each other.

Originally, SDRs were defined in gold; but, inasmuch as they were not actually redeemable in gold, they came to be known as "paper gold."

The optimism expressed by the creators of the new paper gold soon wore thin. In 1974, with the free market price of gold far above the official price, the SDRs were redefined. Instead of being expressed in gold, they were expressed in some sixteen paper currencies, most of which had been depreciating in value for years. Small wonder then that the governors of the International Monetary Fund have difficulty in agreeing upon any basis for allocating them among member nations.

The latest attempt to create monetary stability is the proposal for an international substitution account to mop up unwanted dollars circulating internationally. Although the idea has been embraced with degrees of enthusiasm by member nations of the International Monetary Fund, its usefulness depends on the willingness by creditors to accept a monetary item against an accounting unit, which is defined in terms of Special Drawing Rights. The problem is the lack of willingness by the member nations to put their faith in an item (SDRs) that has proved unusable since its introduction in 1967. Therefore, the substitution account, although it represents an interesting idea, is impractical in terms of utilization.

"Floating" Rates

Another gimmicky cosmetic solution to the deep-rooted monetary problems of the world has been "floating rates." The argument advanced in their behalf is that countries with fixed exchange rates cannot effectively determine their own money supplies and therefore their own price levels. It would be better, so the theory went, for currencies to "float" against each other without any fixed ratios of exchange.

What this system actually does is increase the cost of dealing internationally by increasing the cost of currency contracts. The reason is simple: it has become absolutely essential for international traders of goods or commodities to insure the value of the funds they will receive.

In fact, floating rates not only discourage world trade by adding to costs, but they also generate additional problems. For example, they invite overspeculation in international currencies, as attested by the plight of some of the best-known names in the world banking community. And they also encourage governments to manipulate their currencies to create favorable balance of trade positions without going through the more painful process of making fundamental internal changes in their economies.

Bankers' Problems

The effect of international currency instability on the banking institutions of the world is not to be overlooked. On October 8, 1979, before the American Bankers Association in New Orleans, Comptroller of the Currency John G. Heimann warned that the nation should be prepared to face the failure of some large banks because of the liquidity squeeze resulting from the Federal Reserve's anti-inflation moves. He compared the situation to the conditions that forced the closing of the Franklin National Bank in 1974.

The problems of the Long Island–based Franklin National Bank were once described as untypical of banks as a whole. But it has since become evident that Franklin was just the tip of the iceberg—bank troubles were clearly worldwide. No one could be unduly startled by the goings-on at the Beverly Hills Bancorporation or the United States National Bank of San Diego. But the list of institutions with unexpected problems included the Chase Manhattan Bank, Lloyds Bank of London, and other prestigious names. Early in 1974 Bankhaus Herstatt in Cologne, West Germany, went bankrupt after suffering heavy foreign exchange trading losses, and during the 1977 recession, several smaller European banks were closed.

There is little doubt that the obsession with performance which has afflicted bankers in recent years has now come home to roost. And while some contend that the Federal Reserve could not possibly permit one of the major U.S. banks to go under, Comptroller Heimann appeared to be warning that this confidence is misplaced, and particularly for the hundreds of smaller banks that may become mired in financial difficulty. The overall effect of any sizable rescue operation for banks would surely be highly inflationary.

In retrospect there is little doubt that the "gunslingers" of 1974 were the one-bank holding companies; they were in a position comparable to the youthful stockbrokers who were being hailed as financial geniuses just a few years ago.

This must be remembered: the funds that represent the capital of the banks have their base in fiduciary sources. Yet these acquisitive enterprises have been permitted to enter fields that bear no relation to fiduciary responsibilities—for instance, they have engaged in speculative real estate syndications and high-risk foreign exchange gambits, and have provided the wherewithal for purely speculative corporate takeovers.

Inflation's Manifestations

There is no difficulty in singling out numerous manifestations of inflation in the American economy.

For instance, the East New York Savings Bank in the summer of 1979 offered to give away a brand-new Rolls Royce sedan to any depositor willing to commit $160,000 of funds for deposit for eight years. This represented interest on the deposit at 8 percent per annum, payable in advance, and suitably discounted for early payment. The bank's argument for its bonus plan was to assert—quite correctly—that no one could foresee what a Rolls Royce would cost eight years later, after the interest had accumulated.

We have a long distance to go before the improbable stage where inflation is unbearable, where prices change not monthly or weekly, but day by day and even hour by hour.

But the handwriting is on the wall. We now have escalation clauses in virtually all major labor contracts because unions won't sign up without some assurance that their pay raises won't be wiped out by rising prices.

Because of inflation there is growing occurrence of *indexation*—compensation in just about every financial transaction for the changing rate of inflation. It has already met with some success in Austria, which has adopted an interest bonus scheme calling for extra payments to a lender, equal to the rate of inflation. Brazil seems to have had some success with indexation. More will be said about this inflation-compensation system later in Chapter 11.

Effective anti-inflation measures are still possible even at this late date. But serious moves to control inflation carry with them political risk for officeholders, who are often fearful of moving with the speed and decisiveness that the circumstances call for. Any program to check inflation inevitably increases unemployment and often politically unpalatable economic occurrences. These measures rarely attract politicians, particularly in election years. We cannot count on politicians to act responsibly. Their first priority is to get reelected, even at the price of more inflation.

Americans, naturally, aren't as aware of inflation's perils as are most Europeans. Those Americans who examine photographs of Germans burning worthless marks issued during the Weimar Republic can only feel a sense of curiosity. They are confident it couldn't happen here.

Germans, however, feel quite different. Some can still remember the days in 1923 when a newspaper cost 200 marks, with the price only three months later jumping to 2,000 marks.

At one stage a half-liter of milk went for 250,000 marks; lodgings, 400,000 marks; dinner, 1.8 million marks.

In the summer of 1922, a dollar was worth 575 marks. Only a year later it was worth 1.65 *billion* marks!

Superinflation had a traumatic effect on Germany and helped bring Hitler and Nazism to power, with tragic consequences for the Germans as well as the rest of the world.

The Germans haven't forgotten. That is one reason why West Germany has controlled inflation better than most leading industrial powers in the Western world.

The Role of Gold

But what if the U.S. should get into more serious inflation?

We would then have to prepare for a new currency whose monetary value could be defended. This could be accomplished only with a gold-linked dollar, in combination with a steep rise in the official gold price and a reopening of the gold window for central banks. The gold cover clause would legally require that the U.S. Treasury possess a certain fixed amount of gold in terms of dollar value, not ounces, for the printing of a certain fixed amount of paper currency.

Gold, of course, would not be the only answer to such a dilemma. However, it is the only constituent of the monetary reserves in the Western world with the ability to grow by virtue of price increases.

Historical proof of this was furnished by an agreement entered into by West Germany and Italy in 1974. For purposes of the loan agreement, Italy's gold was valued at the free market price averaged over an eight-week period, or approximately

$120 an ounce. This collateralized value was far in excess of the official U.S. Treasury price of $42.22 per ounce.

Italy, in other words, issued gold-backed promissory notes to obtain a $2 billion credit from the Germans. And the Germans accepted (as collateral) gold valued near the free market price rather than the artificial "official" U.S. Treasury price. For those hoping to minimize gold's importance in international monetary transactions, the German-Italian deal was a shock.

More accommodations of this type may be expected on the international scene, inasmuch as other countries are facing severe financial strain because of soaring oil bills.

One solution—perhaps the only solution at the moment—may be gold-collateralized transactions.

However, a word of caution is in order. The Italian-German agreement, concluded in an atmosphere of crisis, assisted Italy by providing funds needed for its oil purchases. But perhaps historians will conclude that it might have been better for Italy to default on her oil obligations and thus bring pressure on the Arabs to ease their stranglehold on the Free World's economy.

While the use of gold at market-related prices obviously can serve to increase the reserves of a country entering into such an arrangement, the benefits are not all one-sided. As reserves are increased without benefit of a monetary system with controls on the use of such increased reserves, a new "engine" of inflation is created.

This means that even though such agreements do provide an easy way of meeting an emergency situation, such as paying an oil bill, no positive long-term economic benefits are gained unless the agreements are also accompanied by a revised monetary system that acts to control the uses of the newly created reserves.

The solution to the problem, therefore, must start at the root cause. A monetary system must be devised that is sound, viable, and disciplinary—with the help of gold. Not until such a system is devised, and its responsibilities accepted by the international monetary authorities, will the winds of economic trauma and disorder subside.

Chapter 3

Gold as a Gauge
of Anxiety

"It is extraordinary how many emotional storms one may weather in safety if one is ballasted with ever so little gold."

—*William McFee,* Casuals of the Sea

GOLD IS A most peculiar commodity. It cannot be eaten; its utility for actual consumption is so slight that most of the gold ever mined is still in existence. Yet for reasons deeply rooted in the social and economic history of civilization, it is one of the world's most sought-after substances. In a time of change, it is a refuge of stability. Individuals grasping for security reach for gold. Demand for gold is a measure of the world's anxieties.

Since there is not enough gold in the world to serve as a medium of exchange in international trade, the dollar fills that function. In sheer volume, the dollar is the world's leading currency, backed by the resources, the reputation, and the credit of the world's leading trading nation. The rise and fall of the dollar's value is closely related to the level of the world's fears. We saw this effect in the crises in Korea, in the war in Vietnam, and more recently in the religious revolution in Iran. In the long reach of history, military conflict and political upheaval create new levels of anxiety, and anxiety creates new demand for gold.

A demand for gold is closely linked with shortages of more useful commodities like food and fuel. Shortages of true essentials represent limitations on man's freedom and choices. People's anxieties are heightened in times of food shortage; men and women spend much of their time in a struggle merely to stay alive. When fuel is scarce, their physical comfort is impaired and so is their mobility.

During the Indochina war and its aftermath, we saw how once-prosperous families, threatened with imprisonment, starvation, or immediate execution, concentrated their wealth into gold and used it to buy their freedom.

Under less critical conditions, wealthy persons anxious to ensure their futures and those of their children react in much the same way. They seek to preserve and increase their resources, i.e., their security. They tend to shun the more traditional forms of investment—stocks, bonds, real estate—and become purchasers of precious metals.

The causes of anxiety may be of sociopolitical or geopolitical origin, that is, related to shifts in the social structure or in the world power structure. The two often ride in tandem.

In 1929, birth year of the Great Depression, economic error created major sociopolitical change. In the 1970s and probably in the 1980s, sociopolitical change seems likely to generate economic error.

We believe that those who expect a replay of the 1929 crash misread the politics of our time. Following the avalanche of 1929, the controllers of the U.S. economy administered the wrong corrective. They contracted the money supply, worsened the depression, and gave rise to the New Deal, the great bloodless social revolution of our time.

The errors of money management that deepened the depression are not likely to be repeated in the 1980s. Rather the contraction of the economy is likely to produce political and economic measures to relieve the discomfort of growing unemployment and shrinking business activity. Such correctives could produce results as disastrous as those of the early years of the Great Depression. The symptom will not be depression, but uncontrolled inflation.

Karl Marx vs. Capitalism

The man who best understood capitalism was the antithesis of all that capitalism represented. Karl Marx saw clearly that capitalism's greatest strength—its ability to create wealth— was also its weakness. The system that so magnificently creates wealth tends to overcreate, and that overcreation sets the stage for wrongly conceived political decisions.

Inflation arises not just from too many dollars chasing too few goods; it rises also from too many politicians chasing too many votes.

The economy contains many built-in devices for self-correction. Inflation puts pressure on profit margins. Prices move beyond the ability or willingness of consumers to pay. Money becomes expensive, and because of high costs and reduced demand, business tends to contract. A recession results.

If recessions were allowed to progress without interference from the government, the normal safety valves would function. The cost of labor and materials would ease, soon followed by prices, and in time sales would climb, employment rise, and the level of business activity show a healthy surge. Capitalism's axiomatic abundance and the miracle of productivity would in time restore a more positive economic environment.

However, as Marx understood, a recession—or depression—creates an irresistible demand for political action. During every recession we have experienced since the Franklin Roosevelt era, economic fine tuners have engineered expansive fiscal and monetary policies. Government spending was increased, taxes were cut, and the resulting deficits financed by the easy-money policies of the Federal Reserve, all with the goal of reviving economic activity.

Like a drug addict, the economy has required bigger and bigger doses of corrective medicine to achieve the desired results. Each round of economic stimulus produced bigger price increases and smaller gains in healthy economic activity. So the politically expedient steps to cut short recessions have produced a form of stagflation, which we prefer to call *inflession,* suggesting the very real tilt toward inflation and simultaneous recession.

Up the Down Cycle—and Back

The recessions, while they lasted, have caused financial crises among some of the nation's best-known corporations. But some otherwise outspoken advocates of free enterprise have quickly struck their colors rather than face up to the necessary but difficult decisions: to cut back staff, dispose of unprofitable subsidiaries, or even accept corporate liquidation. Some major corporate entities have gone hat in hand to Washington for government assistance. Penn Central, Lockheed, and Chrysler are only the more visible members of this growing parade.

It is understandable that corporate managements and shareholders would seek ways to salvage their enterprises, and not shrink from accepting a government role in the rescue. But it is difficult to square a capitalistic economic philosophy with demands for a government debt subsidy to solve an immediate problem. Further, it is now difficult to believe that any major municipality or key mass transportation industry will ever be allowed to face bankruptcy or liquidation. The close-knit relationships between these major corporations and the banking establishment preclude such a development. Rather the pressures mounted during these periods of inflession-recession tend to form a base for the next logical step, which is to *govern-ism*. This can be identified as a time when national governments take a greater hand in the management of private enterprise through the device of debt guarantees. In fact, it is unavoidable that the federal government must, in fact, stand prepared to guarantee the debts of major corporations, municipalities, or mass transportation industries.

The reason for this is simple. Every level of debt affects the next higher level of debt. Debts are generally categorized as credit risks or interest risks. Credit risk debts stand on the health or weakness or the balance sheet of the corporation or other entity that it represents. Interest risk debt is primarily government paper, in which the chance of default on the principal is remote, but the price moves up and down in response to variations in the interest rates.

If any level of debt fails, be it low or middle level of credit risk, the next higher level of debt encounters difficulty—that difficulty defined as the increased cost of money required in payment of loans obtained. It follows, then, that if these major debtors on the higher-risk side of the credit spectrum should fail, other similar borrowers would experience greater difficulty floating loans and would be forced to pay higher interest rates. The process of government would become both more difficult and more expensive.

It is logical to assume that the natural transition is from capitalism through inflation to recession to inflession and thence into governism. Following governism comes state capitalism. This, in our judgment, is a form of socialism most easily accepted by the once neo-capitalistic world. Not only is it easily accepted, but it appears to be just the form being sought by men high in the corporate and industrial world once regarded as leading defenders of capitalism.

We believe that these trends will continue, despite some contrary indications, such as the election of Conservative governments in Britain and Canada, and the adoption of California's tax-limiting Proposition 13. Political action is influenced less by the liberal-conservative orientation of politicians. In times of business contraction and declining employment, voters are likely to demand expansionary fiscal and monetary policies—that is, actions to increase government spending and deficits, and the creation of new money to meet the demands of government. The politicians are almost sure to oblige. In the short term, these actions do tend to increase employment and real income.

Searching for a Safe Place

The outlook of investors has been affected by the transition from capitalism to state capitalism. This transition is the sociopolitical event that encourages capital to flee. Capital, or accumulated wealth, continues to be produced by enterprises that we associate closely with the capitalistic system. Wealth is not a product of socialism, whose central concern is the distribution, not the creation of wealth. Quite naturally, then, as a society moves away from the capitalistic system, holders of wealth seek a refuge from the rigors of state capitalism. That is a central reason why throughout the once capitalistic world, demand has increased exponentially for tangible assets, which stand to appreciate rather than decline in value.

A look at the changing composition of wealth in Great Britain and Scandinavia as those societies move through this period of transition reveals that wealth is being concentrated in new forms. The new storehouses of value tend to be private, portable, and potentially profitable. That explains why old cars, rare coins, stamps, Chinese porcelains, jades, and a myriad of other tangible items have increased in value. We believe that such tangibles will continue to appreciate in value throughout this period of transition.

Gold itself is only an objective tangible. Its value has increased in part because it, too, represents a private, portable, and potentially appreciating commodity, useful to those seeking to escape what they identify as the hazards of state socialism and the dilution of private property rights that is part of this development.

Along with these sociopolitical trends, we are also seeing a geopolitical transition—a transfer of power—not limited to the Middle East but extending for different reasons into much of the African continent. The key to the Middle East's growing wealth, power, and influence is energy. Africa's potential gains depend to some extent on energy, especially in Nigeria and Angola, but more importantly rest on the array of critical and strategic minerals found in great abundance in the vast plateau of Southern Africa. These materials are principally catalytic and alloy agents that are essential to the functioning of modern societies based on advanced technology.

Our study of the location of the world's supply of some of the more important strategic minerals shows that over 70 percent of the world's supply of these critical materials lies in nations where private property has come under collective ownership or under the direct influence of Communist ideology.

The geopolitical transition in the Middle East, moreover, has all but removed the direct influence of the Free World over the supply, availability, and price predictability of energy. The Islamic revolution in Iran has tended to bring the price of oil under Koranic as well as economic influence.

This growing power of OPEC oil has also been projected into the internal affairs of the U.S. In a suit filed in a U.S. district court, in which the Machinists Union asserted that the price-fixing action of the OPEC cartel violated U.S. law, the Department of Justice took the position that the court lacked jurisdiction, tacitly supporting the OPEC defense. The conclusion to be drawn from these events is that the U.S. government regarded the threat of OPEC retaliation as a more serious matter than the continued operation of a cartel within the U.S.

New Status, New Heights

Both sociopolitical and geopolitical events have affected the pricing and the world movements of gold. The first Nixon administration saw gold in its final days as a direct source of monetary discipline. The existing gold cover clause required the Treasury to maintain a prescribed amount of gold—in value, not in ounces—as backing for the dollar. Then Treasury Secretary John Connally's removal of the gold cover clause effectively demonetized gold, and eliminated it as a form of monetary control. In the next stage, Connally's successor, Treasury Secretary William Simon, relegated gold to the status of a commodity.

Secretary Simon publicly stated his purpose and then, drawing on his experience as one of Wall Street's most skilled traders, accomplished his aims. This completed the relegation of gold from the underpinning of the U.S. currency to a simple commodity. Its next transition was from a commodity to an efficient commodity, bearing a price that is sensitive to market conditions throughout the world. This was accomplished by the institution of gold sales by the International Monetary Fund and the U.S. Treasury. These events, more than any other, led the price of gold into new high territory. The gold auctions allowed substantial interests to enter the market twice a month and buy in volume at a singular price.

Originally, even the suggestion of major official auctions tended to depress the price of gold. When U.S. Treasury sales began on May 23, 1978, gold declined from slightly below 200[1] to 168, then began its rise to the substantial levels it later reached. The character of the Treasury sales was transformed by the presence of the Dresdner Bank, representing Mideast interests. The same bank had previously represented Mideast oil interests in the purchase of sizable blocks of stock in the Krupp and Mercedes industries in West Germany. In the gold auctions, the presence of the Dresdner bank, with its bids for substantially all of the gold offered, demonstrated to the world that gold had indeed become an efficient commodity.

What changed with the entry of the Dresdner Bank and its wealthy principals was market volume. The situation might be compared to one in which an investment adviser presents an investment suggestion to the fund manager of a major securities investment fund. The investment adviser would also have prepared a dossier on the company, its executives, its products, its industry, and its competition. The first question the fund manager asks involves not the company's characteristics or outlook, but the number of shares outstanding and the average daily trading volume in its stock. If the trading volume is low, the fund manager would be likely to dismiss the stock from consideration, except for personal accounts. The fund would not be able to enter the market without disrupting prices.

Similarly, if the gold market had remained a low-volume operation, overly sensitive to small transactions, it is unlikely that Mideast nations which now represent the bulk of demand would have adopted gold as an investment medium. The introduction of large-volume sales from the International Monetary Fund and United States Treasury auctions made it possible for the oil-rich interests from the Middle East to enter the market in large volume, and yet complete substantially planned purchases in a single day at a single price. The next and possibly final step in the evolution of gold was its return to a role in the

[1]That is, $200 per ounce of gold.

monetary systems. Demonetization is the removal of gold from monetary reserves; remonetization is its restoration to such a role. With the establishment of ECU (European Currency Unit), the currency form of the European monetary system, gold was adopted as a constituent item in the reserves of this new currency form. That constituted the remonetization of gold, so far as the group of European currencies is concerned.

A Warning From the Sheik

The U.S., which benefits from the use of its dollars as an international reserve currency for the pricing and payment of commodities including gold and oil, got a strong warning from one of its good friends in the Arab world to halt the erosion of the dollar's value. Sheik Yamani, oil minister of Saudi Arabia, pointedly warned in June 1979 that if the U.S. dollar declined by as much as 5 percent from its then existing value, Saudi Arabia would propose to the other OPEC members to abandon the dollar as the sole pricing mechanism for oil. OPEC is believed to be studying the creation of a new pricing device, based on the weighted value of a group of currencies, plus gold. Settlements would continue to be made in dollars, possibly in combination with pounds sterling. If the basket-of-currencies device is adopted as an oil pricing yardstick, this would seriously erode the prestige and value of the dollar on foreign exchange markets and give a new surge to the price of gold.

There are other suggestions that large international traders are beginning to bypass the dollar, the traditional medium for international payments. South Africa, which long depended on Iran as its principal supplier of oil, found itself cut off from that source by an arbitrary embargo declared by the new revolutionary government of Iran. While South Africa has not confirmed the details of its new source of supply, it is reported to have made direct gold-for-oil barter arrangements with other Middle East suppliers, either Saudi Arabia or the United Arab Emirates, or both. Although South Africa is stockpiling oil against the possibility of a new embargo, there are no obvious signs of fuel shortage in that sternly independent republic.

While payments for these major shipments of oil were made directly in gold, the sales were denominated in dollars, and the large transfers of gold were believed to be behind a sharp surge in the price of gold, from 248 to 280. This in turn set the stage for another major rally in gold that took the price from 282 to 375 in the short space of six weeks. During that time the U.S. dollar remained somewhat weak, but relatively stable against other major currencies. These gold-for-oil deals were the probable cause for gold's price rise, since no other obvious factor was involved.

As we see it, the substitution of gold for dollars in international settlements marks the final stage of the remonetization of gold. The movement out of dollars into gold may have been triggered by a desire for oil-wealthy Mideast nations or individuals to diversify 5 to 10 percent of their holdings out of dollars into precious metals. The transition in the West from capitalism to a form of state socialism was at least in part behind this move; it finally impressed the holders of substantial wealth in the OPEC countries.

This final transition, it seems to us, puts a foundation under the price of gold at the levels prevailing in the final quarter of 1979. Most certainly, the price of gold will continue to fluctuate, but rather than having seen a peak, we believe we are witnessing a shift into a major bull phase whose high point has not yet been attained.

Chapter 4

American Ownership of Bullion

"People fight the gold standard because they want to substitute national autarchy for free trade, war for peace, totalitarian government omnipotence for liberty."

—*Ludwig von Mises*

ON AUGUST 14, 1974, President Gerald Ford signed a bill allowing American citizens to buy and sell gold on and after December 31, 1974. Many believed that this event would not be allowed to take place. In fact, for some inexplicable reason, Dr. Arthur F. Burns, chairman of the Federal Reserve Board, waited until just prior to legalization to say, "it is my duty to point out that prompt removal of present restrictions on private trading in gold could complicate a financial situation that is already beset by strains and stresses."

Nevertheless, the most momentous event to affect gold in nearly half a century did take place, and the result was a disappointment for those who had expected fireworks.

The initial American reaction was one of apathy, and, as one London dealer described it, "the whole thing came off like a slightly damp squib," the British equivalent of a wet firecracker.

What happened?

The explanation seems clear. In anticipation of heavy demand from American gold buyers, the price of gold was pushed up to what was then an all-time high of $197.50 an ounce on December 30, just one day before Americans could legally buy the yellow metal. When American demand failed to meet expectations, investors and speculators rushed to bail out and the result was a steep slide in the price of gold to an inter-day low of $101.50.

The lack of American interest in gold in the period immediately following legalization can, in our judgment, be attributed to four factors:

1. The anticipatory price rise in gold just prior to "G-day" when American ownership was legalized.

2. The well-publicized Treasury announcement that it would auction two million ounces of gold, worth about $380 million at prevailing market prices, less than a week after the legalization date.

3. The disclosure that many major banking institutions, such

as the Bank of America, Pittsburgh's Mellon Bank, and New York's Chase Manhattan and Morgan Guaranty Trust had decided not to offer gold at retail at that time, though some of the banks are considering changes in policy in this regard.

4. Warnings from a host of official and unofficial sources concerning gold's price volatility, high acquisition cost, and other risk factors.

A Healthy Beginning?

We are convinced that the failure of a buying panic to develop in the initial phases of gold trading in the United States was healthy for the future of gold ownership by Americans. Nothing dampens the ardor of a speculator or investor more than buying at the top of a price rise and then being obliged to sit with paper losses for many months. Fortunately, Americans proved to be more canny traders than some Europeans had expected and didn't rush in to buy gold at the then highest prices on record.

Incidentally, many observers overlooked the fact that impressive activity took place in the futures market, where the volume of gold futures contracts was the highest for any opening day of a new contract on U.S. exchanges.

We have long contended that it would be most unfortunate if the American merchandising miracle that led to mass consumption of soap, cigarettes, and deodorants became so pervasive that it branched out to include gold. Slick promotion may be fine for household necessities, but when it's aimed at encouraging gold ownership it would be self-defeating. It could only result in bringing many people into the gold market who do not understand the nature of the metal—and ultimately this would have negative consequences.

United States vs. Japan

Some skeptics have noted that in Japan a short-run buying spurt soon faded after gold ownership was legalized—and they have predicted that a similar pattern will emerge in this country. However, in evaluating the interest of Japanese investors in gold, it must be emphasized that, historically, the Japanese have displayed a stronger interest in *platinum* than have Westerners. Also, it seems clear that the failure of Japanese suppliers to "make a market" in gold bars made it difficult for investors to resell their gold, and, naturally, this helped to dampen the demand for gold.

Obviously, the American situation is quite different from that of major European countries where the purchase of gold has been compared to stopping off at the butcher's shop to pick up a pound of meat for the dinner table. America will not become another France or India overnight.

It also must be kept in mind that, even while the decades-old prohibition against gold ownership remained in effect, some Americans found ways to satisfy their desire for the yellow metal. For instance, they could buy gold coins, jewelry, the shares of gold mining companies, and other forms of gold-related investments.

They also dabbled illegally in gold purchases. No one can offer more than an educated guess, but some authorities have estimated the value of gold held by Americans in banks outside the U.S. prior to legalization at anywhere from $5 billion to $10 billion.

Americans are not by habit gold hoarders; they apparently turn to gold only when other values appear to be threatened with collapse. In contrast, the French, after centuries of war, revolution, and currency devaluations, have learned to love gold. It is estimated that the French account for the largest percentage of privately held gold in Europe. It would have taken a bold forecaster to predict that Americans, in the first year of legalization, would develop the same passion for gold that has become traditional in other parts of the world.

But who is to say that American psychology is immune to change, particularly if a great number of people become convinced that the United States is on the brink of serious monetary and economic problems?

This is the enigma faced by forecasters seeking to assess future demand for gold by Americans.

It should be borne in mind that gold is not so much an investment as a speculation. It cannot be considered a pure investment because it produces no current interest return for the holder. Actually, the lack of any return on the investment, plus storage and insurance charges and possibly a premium for purchases in small quantities, results in a negative return for the holder. A rough rule of thumb is to add somewhere around 15 to 20 percent per year to the nominal purchase price to reflect these charges at today's cost of money.

Then, too, remember that the physical gold market—unlike the gold futures market and other securities exchanges —is almost totally unregulated. The Securities & Exchange Commission, though it emphasizes that all sales of gold aren't necessarily exempt from securities laws, and that it will be closely scrutinizing future developments, has also indicated that it doesn't consider gold sales by banks and brokerage firms as being subject to regulation in the same manner as securities.

This means that the prospective gold buyer must follow the rule of *caveat emptor* and be sure that he is dealing with a reputable firm, preferably one that has been in business for a long time. (If you aren't sure, check with your bank or Better Business Bureau.) Avoid doing business with a hastily organized one-man "mint," which may resort to bait advertising in leading newspapers and magazines. It is unfortunate but true that sometimes the most unscrupulous do the most advertising. Avoid any firm selling gold or gold-related investments through fear tactics.

Banks, brokerage firms, coin and bullion dealers, private mints, jewelers, and many other outlets have been ready to supply gold since the ban on American ownership was lifted. Some of the offerings, of course, may be considered as novelties rather than as investments. For instance, one leading New York jeweler sells gold pendants bearing the store's well-known name and the weight of the pieces (⅛ oz., ¼ oz., ½ oz. or a full ounce), but the retail prices of the items are about 60 percent higher than their value as bullion, not counting New York sales tax. They may be attractive objects for display or conversation pieces, but anyone seeking to resell these expensive gimmicks at anything close to cost would face a king-size headache.

Brokerage Houses

The serious gold buyer would do well to consider the services of leading stock brokerage firms that have entered the gold business. For instance, Merrill Lynch, Pierce, Fenner & Smith and Bache Halsey Stuart Shields, Inc., among others, have established programs for dealing in gold. James Sinclair Commodities, a New York City–based firm of which one of the authors of this book is a general partner, has facilities to handle orders for either gold bullion or gold coins at competitive prices, adjusted in accord with world markets.

Typically, brokerage customers will pay the London market's opening price for the morning following the buyer's order. (The opening price, which is known as the London Bullion Fix, is issued at 5:30 A.M., New York time.) Gold may be sold on the same terms that it is bought: the London market price for the following morning, less the broker's charge. Some dealers transact at market-related prices during trading hours for Hong Kong, as well as for the London, New York, and Chicago markets, providing service up to eighteen hours a day.

In order to be competitive, brokers must offer gold that bears a well-known assay mark. They should offer to deliver gold to the customer's bank for safekeeping or else provide the machinery whereby gold can be stored and the buyer provided with a document similar to a warehouse receipt.

The New York Stock Exchange has taken steps to facilitate gold and silver dealings by its member firms. The Exchange has authorized member firms to buy and sell bullion for clients on margin arrangements which are largely at the discretion of the firms themselves, provided only that the metal is properly stored, secured, and insured. Purchases fully paid for within five business days are treated as cash transactions.

Banks and Gold

New York's Republic National Bank has been one of the banking institutions most active in the selling of gold to both large-scale industrial users and to retail buyers. Customers may buy gold in one-half ounce, one-ounce, one-kilo (32.151 oz.), or 400-ounce bars, for the spot price of gold plus a commission of 2¾ percent and a storage fee of $1.20 per ounce per year.

The First National Bank of Chicago offers its customers a program for the accumulation of gold, starting with a minimum of five ounces, offered at a spot price plus 2 percent, and a storage fee of ⅛ of 1 percent per quarter. Later additions to the account may be made in amounts of one ounce or more, and the customer is given a passbook, something like a savings account record, to show his deposits. First Chicago also deals in gold coins, and in bars of gold in sizes ranging from one-fourth ounce up to one kilo.

One handicap banks face is the lack of regulations governing their handling of gold or widely accepted techniques for dealing in the retail market for bullion. As you can see from the preceding paragraphs, each bank tends to develop its own techniques and rules. And some bankers have been anxious to avoid the appearance of promoting gold sales at the expense of more traditional investments.

The banking industry has taken a generally cautious attitude toward dealing in gold. A number of the largest banks, notably including the nation's biggest, Bank of America, and New York's Bankers Trust and Chase Manhattan, do not make retail sales of gold, although Chase will oblige a trust customer who wishes to purchase bullion for investment. Pittsburgh's Mellon Bank explained that it feared the promotion of gold sales "might induce speculation by individuals who don't have a clear understanding of the risks involved."

However, other banks—such as New York's Citibank—offer a variety of gold-based investments. Citibank markets the newly issued Canadian Maple Leaf coin, which contains one ounce of .999 fine gold, and may have some minor numismatic value as well as its bullion value, since the government of Canada plans to limit coinage in the first three years of its issue to 5,000,000 units. Citibank also sells gold certificates with a minimum opening value of $1,000. On receiving an order for a $1,000 certificate, the bank deducts a 3 percent commission, then checks the market for the maximum amount of gold that the remaining $970 will buy, and makes the purchase for the customer. Later purchases may be added in amounts as small as $100. On request, the bank will deliver the amount of gold in the customer's account from its depository in London, in Zurich, or in Delaware, which has no state sales tax. Citibank's gold purchase services are also available to customers of correspondent banks.

Bankers, of course, are worried that some unsophisticated customers may hold banks responsible if they are unable to sell gold at the price they originally paid for it. The banks are also concerned over the lack of qualified personnel, and of course they can hardly be expected to welcome large-scale withdrawal of funds from checking and time accounts during a period of credit stringency.

Still, banks must be regarded as a logical marketing force in gold transactions now that they have overcome their initial hesitancy. They can lend money to buy gold, lend money against gold as collateral, and they can store the metal—all of which can generate worthwhile income for the banks as volume develops.

Group Ownership

Several vehicles, set up along investment company lines, have been proposed to enable investors to join together in buying gold on a group basis. While the principle of group ownership may have some merit, because in some cases the investor can avoid assaying, fabrication, and shipping fees as well as sales taxes, each plan should be carefully judged on its own merits. The tax status, minimum initial investment, and fees levied by the respective organizations are all matters to be carefully considered.

Principles to Follow

For prospective buyers of gold, in large or small quantities, this general advice is offered:

1. Check the reputation of the individual or organization through whom you are buying or selling gold—if there is any doubt, take your business elsewhere.

2. Make sure that any gold bullion you buy bears the mark of a known refiner, assaying weight and fineness. *Ask for a written guarantee.* (Engelhard Minerals & Chemicals Corporation, for instance, is a well-known refiner which offers gold in bars up to 400 troy ounces, with its own stamp and in distinctive shapes.)

3. Keep in mind that the offering price to you will, of necessity, reflect a commission for the seller of gold. If the commission seems too high, it would pay to "shop around" for a better buy. A rough rule of thumb is that the commission or markup shouldn't exceed 5 percent for physical delivery. Obviously you will pay a higher commission rate on small quantities of gold than on large purchases.

4. Be wary of any deals in which the seller stipulates that the customer is required to resell bullion back to him. This could mean that the price you may eventually receive will be determined by the seller, and his price could differ markedly from prevailing market quotations.

5. Be extremely cautious if you purchase gold bullion or coins on margin. You may be able to get in on as little as 10 percent

margin, but you would be in an extremely vulnerable position in the event that the gold price declines and you are unable (or unwilling) to put up additional margin. It has come to light that certain unethical dealers offering margin arrangements in the trading of Krugerrands (the popular South African gold coins) have in fact failed to buy the underlying Krugerrands, resulting in their inability to deliver in rising markets. If one chooses to use leverage, it is advisable to work through an organized exchange and not a private company. If the leverage is provided by a private company, the safety of your investment depends upon the strength of the balance sheet and the legitimacy of the people involved in the private company. In an organized exchange, the clearinghouse function provides for the collection of money every night from those who lose and the payment to those who win; this provides a degree of safety to investors otherwise not available.

6. Remember that the U.S. Treasury will be keeping an eye on traders seeking to use gold transactions as a device for tax avoidance. The government may have difficulty in keeping track of buyers and sellers, but don't count on it.

7. There are a number of unresolved questions concerning the tax status of investment vehicles that are designed to purchase gold in a group plan. If you go this route, seek qualified advice.

8. Generally speaking, it is preferable not to take delivery of gold, except in small quantities. It is simpler and less expensive to let a refiner or broker store your gold and provide you with a document similar to a warehouse receipt, attesting to your ownership. You will also avoid the cost of having your gold re-assayed when you want to sell it.

9. If you decide to accept delivery of gold, seek to do so outside a high sales-tax state. Arrangements for out-of-state delivery, entirely legal, can be made through your bank or broker.

10. The purchase of very small amounts of gold, such as one-tenth ounce wafers, except as gifts or mementoes, is not very practical. You will pay a substantial premium on purchase and a commission when you sell, and these fees will absorb most of your profits, if any, on the entire transaction.

Chapter 5

Fundamentals
of
Futures Markets

"I'm very scared at what's happening now—the trend at present is leading to hell."
        —*Dr. Gunnar Myrdal, quoted in October 1974*
        upon receipt of the Nobel Prize in Economics

A FUTURES CONTRACT is a legally binding instrument to buy or sell a designated quantity of a given commodity, at a specific time in the future, at a price agreed upon today. The contract will outline the standards that the commodity must meet to be acceptable for delivery.

Each commodity exchange has specific trading units, namely minimum standard quantities of the commodities it trades. For example, the minimum quantity in silver futures contracts on the New York Commodity Exchange is 5,000 ounces.

Typically, a commodity speculator is required by a commodity brokerage firm to provide a deposit or "margin" of approximately 5 percent to 20 percent before executing the order. But it is interesting to note that a speculator rarely lets the contract mature. It has been estimated that less than 3 percent of all contracts entered into in the futures markets are actually delivered.

What the speculator does is "cover" the original contract before it matures by assuming a position equal and opposite to the original trade. The liquidating trade has to be executed on the same exchange as the original contract and must be for the same delivery month.

Thus, if you *bought* 10,000 ounces of silver for delivery in December 1979, you would have covered by *selling* 10,000 ounces for delivery in December 1979.

Two Main Groups

Basically, there are two principal groups of participants who are active in futures trading: speculators and hedgers. The speculators (a classification that includes most of the public) are interested solely in price changes—they buy futures contracts if they think prices will go up and sell futures contracts if they think prices will decline.

The hedger, on the other hand, is usually involved in the

production, processing, or marketing of a particular commodity and employs futures contracts as a tool for financial management purposes. In the case of gold, those who hedge would include miners, smelters, and fabricators of the metal.

Until the lifting of the forty-one-year ban on private ownership of gold in the United States, trading in gold futures was strictly illegal for Americans. But the ban ended December 31, 1974, and interest in gold futures has been rising apace. American commodity exchanges are trading gold futures contracts, typically for 100 ounces of gold. (Spot contracts are for 400 troy ounces.)

On a standard 100-troy-ounce contract, worth about $40,000 (at a price of $400 an ounce of gold), you would be expected to put down a minimum "security deposit" or margin of about 10 percent, or roughly $4,000. But you most likely would have to put up a larger margin unless you are well known to a commodity brokerage firm—perhaps 16 percent. That is all to the good, because you would be in an extremely vulnerable position with a 10 percent margin. It's a good idea *not* to use all of your leverage when trading in a volatile commodity like gold.

Your costs would include your broker's commission (in the neighborhood of $65 on a "round turn" transaction), storage charges of between $2 and $5 per month for a 100-troy-ounce delivery, plus nominal insurance charges of about 50¢ per $1,000.

Now that trading in gold futures is a reality, such futures trading has become the most popular method of speculating in gold. And since the United States has more mature futures markets than Western Europe, not to mention the world's largest number of potential speculators, the United States is the world headquarters for forward trading of the yellow metal.

London will retain its preeminent position as the main "commodity" market for the metal, serving gold users with the well-oiled machinery, expertise, and tradition that enables the British capital effectively to handle large-scale receipts and deliveries of gold.

Zurich will continue to be a monetary center for gold, serving the needs and desires of those who are motivated by gold for its monetary aspects. It is suited for this, due to the neutrality of Switzerland in world conflicts, its history of money-exchange handling, its nonpolitical protection of asset privacy, and its 800 years of monetary stability.

Considering that Americans have long been accustomed to dealing in a wide range of commodities (corn, wheat, soybeans, etc.) for future delivery, it seems unlikely that any major obstacles will arise to hinder the growth of forward trading of gold. In fact, some of the same exchanges on which futures trading in agricultural commodities is well established provide the market place for trading gold futures. So the United States should quickly catch up with London bullion dealers and Swiss banks that have been handling futures transactions in gold since 1954.

However, forward trading of gold is unlikely to follow exactly the same pattern as futures trading in more conventional commodities. For instance, there is little doubt that a fairly sizable percentage of forward buyers will take delivery of their gold when the contracts mature, assuming continued political uncertainty.

Those who are willing to assume a high degree of risk in return for large potential rewards will find the gold futures market a challenging and stimulating outlet for a portion of their speculative funds. However, some words of caution are in order. Remember that this is a highly volatile market, best suited for those who have ample risk capital at their disposal, as well as nerves of steel. Some knowledge of futures trading (or access to those with expertise in this area) is highly desirable. And be sure to know the people with whom you deal, as there is bound to be some risk of fraud. You don't want to wake up some day and find you are holding a bar of lead covered with a thin layer of gold!

The Winnipeg Market

Gold futures trading has been conducted by the Winnipeg Commodity Exchange since 1972. Some observers have contended that the failure of this market place (which for many years has provided a market for trading in contracts for future delivery of Canadian grains, oil seeds, cattle, and produce) to generate much excitement in gold may have negative implications for speculative interest in gold futures trading.

This conclusion, however, is not necessarily a valid one. The original Winnipeg gold contract covered the standard 400-ounce international bar; thus 400 ounces at $400 an ounce would mean an investment of $160,000.

GOLD FUTURES CONTRACTS AT FIVE MAJOR U.S. EXCHANGES

	Commodity Exchange Inc.	New York Mercantile Exchange	Chicago Board of Trade	Chicago Mercantile Exchange	MidAmerica Commodity Exchange (Chicago)
Contract unit	100 troy oz. (5% tolerance)	32.151 tr. oz. (1 kg.); 400 oz.	96.45 tr. oz. (three 1 kg. bars)	100 troy oz. (5% tolerance)	33.2 oz.
Trading months	Feb., April, June, Aug., Oct., Dec.	Jan., March, May, July, Sept., Dec.	Jan., March, May, July, Sept., Nov.	Jan., March, June, Sept., Dec.	March, June, Sept., Dec.
Deliverable grade	not less than .995 fineness—all exchanges				
Trading hours (Eastern time)	9:45–2:10	9:25–2:30	9:45–2:30	8:50–1:10	8:25–1:40

Source: *The New York Times.*

This contract apparently was too large to generate widespread investment or speculative interest, and evidently the Winnipeg Exchange came around to the same conclusion. It introduced a 100-ounce contract.

No use in trying to sell a Cadillac when the potential buyer is oriented toward a Chevrolet!

Exchanges Dealing in Futures

Among the exchanges actively dealing in gold futures are the following:

1. The Commodity Exchange (COMEX) in New York.
2. The Chicago Board of Trade.
3. The Chicago Mercantile Exchange (International Monetary Market).
4. The MidAmerica Commodity Exchange in Chicago.
5. The New York Mercantile Exchange.

Details of contracts on these exchanges are provided in the table on p. 59.

With the services provided by these and other exchanges, the would-be purchaser of gold futures should have no difficulty in obtaining access to the facilities he requires. With members of these exchanges, the major Swiss banks (as well as many smaller Swiss institutions), London bullion dealers, leading Canadian banks (such as the Bank of Nova Scotia), and others serve the individual's needs.

European banks, generally speaking, will be trading gold futures contracts while American banks will be restricted to dealing in actuals.

For those who understand the risk-reward ratios inherent in gold futures trading, and are willing to accept those risks, the following points should be considered:

1. The most attractive exchange for the investor is the one with the smallest size contract, the largest daily price change limit, and the greatest liquidity.

2. An investor should deal with a member broker of one of the exchanges dealing in gold, or with a broker who has a reciprocating agreement.

3. Be sure, however, to pick a reliable broker, with access to a variety of trading markets, who is cognizant of all aspects of gold. It will cost you no more to do so, since the price of the metal for future delivery is expected to be based on the closing

London gold price, plus a premium that will be governed by the interest rates prevailing for the currency in which the transaction is made.

Incidentally, it is well to remember that regardless of where your futures contract is executed, an exchange itself does no business in the commodities that are traded by its members. Its main function is to provide a center or meeting place where buyers and sellers conduct their business and make contact with other parties involved in the movement and marketing of the commodities in which they are interested.

Effect on the Gold Market

What will be the effect on the gold market now that futures trading has begun?

The answer can only be an educated guess, but the long-term impact should certainly be a positive one for bulls of gold. Some of the yellow metal will have to be made available for those who take actual delivery of gold.

The buyer of gold is likely to have more than a passing interest in foreign currencies. One should not forget that a currency with a gold backing, such as the Swiss franc (officially worth .21759 grams of fine gold), indirectly provides the purchaser with an interest in gold. To some extent, this is true for all of the currencies of the European monetary system[1], whose joint backing includes 84.5 million ounces of gold. Sophisticated traders tend to shift back and forth between gold and the world's stronger currencies.

International currency futures contracts also attract speculative interest. These are contracts that call for the purchase or sale of a specified quantity of a particular currency at a future date. When entered into by the gold trader, they can offer additional opportunities for profits, because of the arbitrage possibilities in conjunction with dealings in the metal.

For instance, assume, now that gold dealing is being legalized, that a one-year futures contract for gold is selling in London at the same level as a one-year futures contract in New York. At the same time, sterling is selling at a sizable discount from the dollar.

It is possible to capitalize on this situation by setting up an

[1]The Deutsche mark, French franc, Italian lira, Belgian franc, Dutch guilder, and Irish pound.

arbitrage. In effect, you can buy gold with discounted sterling and thus acquire gold at a discounted price.

Another trading technique that may be employed is a "straddle," which is sometimes referred to as a "spread" or "switch." This involves the simultaneous purchase of one future month against the sale of another future month of the same commodity. A straddle trade is based on a price relationship between the two months and a belief that the spread, or difference in price, between the two contract months will change sufficiently to make the trade profitable.

Example one: Assume that a person sees near-term tightness in the silver market. In the case of a nonperishable commodity like silver, the difference in the cost of delivery between one month and another should under normal market conditions reflect the cost of carrying the metal, i.e., interest, storage, and insurance.

But in a period of exaggerated near-term demand, the normal premium that reflects the carrying charges may disappear as buyers prove willing to absorb the carrying costs. Under such circumstances, spot silver could actually sell at a premium over forward months.

Example two: The carrying cost of gold consists almost entirely of interest, since storage costs for gold are low, i.e., $3.65 a year for a 100-ounce bar. If a buyer expects both interest rates and the price of gold to rise, he can sell a near-month contract and buy a more distant contract. If his expectations are realized, the value of his distant-month contract will rise, due to higher costs for interest or for the commodity itself or both, and the trader will show a profit when he clears his contracts.

Where Currencies Are Traded

Following World War II the exchange rates among Free World nations were governed by the Bretton Woods Agreement of 1944, which helped to minimize currency fluctuations around fixed exchange rates. The world's central banks set up a system to keep exchange rates for the U.S. dollar within a 1 percent range above or below a declared par value. But with the collapse of the agreement in 1971, there evolved a so-called "floating rate" system. This entailed much greater variability and volatility in rates, inasmuch as the central banks, under a floating rate system, do not protect either the upper or lower currency fluctuation limits.

As we noted in Chapter 2, this has meant serious risks for multinational countries and others engaged in international business operations. For example, if an importer bringing in goods from the Netherlands settles his debts through the purchase of Dutch guilders with U.S. dollars, and if the dollar should decline relative to the guilder during the transaction, he might wind up with a loss instead of a profit.

This is the reason that importers, exporters, financial institutions, and others must protect themselves against the risks associated with widely fluctuating "floating" exchange rates. International currency futures contracts can be quite useful in this regard.

There are several major markets for trading international currencies.

The International Monetary Market of Chicago was set up in 1972 to trade contracts in various kinds of currencies.

The New York Mercantile Exchange has set these minimum and maximum fluctations in connection with the individual currency units:

	Minimum Fluctuation		Maximum Variation	
	per currency	per contract	per currency	per contract
British pound sterling	.0005¢	$12.50	.05¢	$1250
Dutch guilder	.0001¢	12.50	.01¢	1250
Deutsche mark	.0001¢	12.50	.01¢	1250
Swiss franc	.0001¢	12.50	.015¢	1875
Japanese yen	.000001¢	12.50	.01¢	1250
Canadian dollar	.01¢	10.00	.75¢	750
Mexican peso	.00001¢	10.00	.0015¢	1500
French franc	.00005¢	12.50	.005¢	1250

Later, the New York Mercantile Exchange also instituted trading in futures contracts in a number of key foreign currencies. The following contracts are currently traded:

Currency	Unit
British pound sterling	£25,000
Canadian dollar	CAN $100,000
Deutsche mark	DM 125,000
Dutch guilder	HFL 125,000
Japanese yen	Y12,500,000

It should be recognized that, together with the opportunities, there are sizable risks in trading foreign currencies. This activity, in fact, has been likened to Russian roulette. Some well-known banks have lost hundreds of millions of dollars in playing this market, and they are supposed to be experts at it!

Still, for those individuals who are willing and able to assume the risks of fluctuating exchange rates in the hope of potential profit, the opportunities can be quite interesting. Consider, for example, that the nearest future delivery contract for the Deutsche mark traded as low as .5220 in early October 1978 and as high as .5864 before the month was out. This nominal increase of 12.3 percent, however, offered the opportunity of a profit of more than 400 percent in that month to a leveraged trader. It should also be pointed out that after President Carter announced a series of moves to strengthen the dollar on Nov. 1, 1978, the market headed in the opposite direction, exposing traders who overstayed the market to equally spectacular losses.

Still, even in less turbulent times, an individual might feel that the dollar would weaken against the Swiss franc. It would, therefore, be logical to sell dollars short and buy Swiss francs. This could be done by instructing a Swiss bank to purchase francs amounting to the equivalent of $100,000 for delivery in twelve months.

A customer would mail a check to the bank for a 20 percent margin, or $20,000, which the bank would credit to a non-interest-bearing margin account. The bank would sell the client Swiss francs equivalent to $100,000. The sale would take place at the twelve-month forward rate and the customer would pay slightly more than if he bought Swiss francs for immediate delivery.

On the due date the client can either cancel out the contract, or he can roll over the contract for another period of one to twelve months. That is, assuming he has not sold back his francs to the bank before the due date of the contract.

This type of currency futures contract, in effect, offers the possibility of acquiring a claim for the equivalent of $100,000 in Swiss francs with a down payment of $20,000.

Incidentally, forward currency contracts can be obtained not only in Swiss francs, but in Deutsche marks, French francs, Spanish pesetas, Dutch guilders, or pounds sterling—provid-

ing, of course, that each contract exceeds $100,000 or its equiva-
lent.

Another way of playing the shifts in foreign currency rates
is through the purchase of three-month or six-month Swiss
franc certificates of deposit at a Dutch or German bank where
the going rates of interest are substantially higher than those
prevailing in Swiss institutions for the Swiss franc.

These certificates of deposit (CDs) can be denominated in
any currency. Thus an individual who felt that the Swiss franc
was due for an eventual rise could purchase a CD in that currency; in addition to the possible increase in value arising from
the hoped-for increase in value of the franc, the purchaser
would also receive a reasonably attractive interest return on
his investment. Of course, if a currency loses value after purchase the holder will wind up showing a loss on the transaction.

Chapter 6

Role of International Banks in Gold Trading

"I have been accused of being worried over this inflation. I wasn't worried. I was just confused. . . . When you are worried, you know what you are worried about, but when you are confused you don't know enough about a thing to be worried."

—Will Rogers

MORE AMERICANS THAN ever before are making non-traditional types of investments—gold coins, silver, gems, foreign currencies, stamps, works of art, and so on. The trend reflects a number of influences, including investor expectations of the future course of inflation, disenchantment with the results of equity investments, and even a desire to avoid government impediments to the free transfer of their funds.

As they have become more sophisticated in their financial dealings, many Americans have opened Swiss and other international bank accounts for the first time. The number is difficult to estimate.

Their mounting interest is justified by past history. The performance of the Swiss franc against gold—or against virtually any other financial yardstick, for that matter—has been exemplary for more than a century. While runaway inflation ravaged most European economies and hyperinflation destroyed the German mark in the 1919–24 period, the Swiss franc remained immune to the monetary debauchery all around it, and closely maintained its value against gold.

During the 1921–34 period, when banks collapsed like tenpins all over Europe and more than 14,000 U.S. banks failed, only one minor Swiss investment bank became insolvent.

Opening An Account

Those who wish to open a Swiss bank account will find it a simple matter, depending, of course, on the particular bank. It should be emphasized that it is perfectly legal for any U.S. citizen to establish a bank account in Switzerland; all that is required is to indicate the existence of such an account on your U.S. income tax return.

The "Big Three' in the Swiss banking industry are the country's three largest institutions—the Union Bank of Switzerland, the Swiss Bank Corporation, and the Swiss Credit Bank. In addition, among the more than 400 Swiss institutions, there are a number of medium-sized and smaller banks with expertise in serving international clients.

It is interesting to note that Swiss banks, generally speaking, do not solicit American customers—that is not their way of doing business. Nevertheless they have an impressive range of banking capabilities, including some that a good many American banks tend to lack.

For instance, some Americans have begun to invest in foreign currencies in much the same way that many professionals do—namely instructing their banks to roll over (or keep reinvesting) their funds in short term Eurocurrency time deposits or certificates of deposit, denominated in hard currencies like the Swiss franc, the mark, and the guilder.

Trading foreign currencies in this manner carries risks, but in times of currency turmoil it has proven an effective means of safeguarding—and even adding to—one's capital. Importantly, it provides diversification of assets.

Besides offering protection in a crisis, a Swiss bank can transfer your currency from country to country—just about anywhere. In fact many Swiss banking institutions issue checkbooks that enable the drawer of the check to pay in any currency he may desire. This is extremely useful at times of fluctuating exchange rates. For instance, it can enable a traveler to pay his bills in the currency that offers him the most favorable rate at a given time.

Of course the Swiss banks also offer complete privacy in banking transactions, which an individual may find desirable from the standpoint of his personal and family relationships.

Unless you are a heroin dealer or an international swindler, you need have no concern whatsoever that anyone will tamper with the privacy of a Swiss bank account.

Swiss banking is business-oriented, and in no way politically motivated. This is a key to its success. Unlike North America and the other European countries, Swiss bankers, from the central bank down, are career bankers, never political appointees, so they don't come under political pressure. There is no general manager of a big Swiss bank who is also a member of parliament.

Contrary to the belief held in some quarters, Swiss bank accounts normally pay interest.[1] Although the rate may be lower

---

[1]A penalty rate of interest has been levied by the Swiss. It is a measure of

than that obtainable in some U.S. money-market instruments, it has this additional feature: if the Swiss franc—widely recognized as one of the sturdiest currencies in the world—should appreciate against the U.S. dollar, the account holder would have the possibility of significant capital enhancement. Needless to say, there is also downside risk in such transactions.

Thus the Swiss banks can be useful to any actual or potential investor. They can provide expert counsel on foreign investments—including gold—both as a broker and an investment adviser. Their perspective incidentally is not limited to one market, but takes in the entire international investment scene.

It is true that certain other countries (such as the Bahamas, the Cayman Islands, Bermuda, Singapore, etc.) also offer numbered accounts. But the political and economic stability of these countries is not in the same league with that of Switzerland.

In Switzerland, banks are subject to stringent regulations. Cash liquidity requirements approximate 15 percent of total deposits and this total must be readily available for depositors. Banks, moreover, can increase their loans by only 7 percent per annum. Such high cash liquidity, plus strict limits on loan expansion, goes a long way toward ensuring the stability and solvency of the Swiss banking institutions.

Investors who are concerned about bank liquidity these days (and rightfully so) can check three main points in the financial statement of a domestic, Swiss, or other foreign banking institution:

1. As an indicator of cash liquidity, make sure that the bank's actual cash position and due-from-banks at-sight are higher than the due-to-banks at-sight item on the liability side of the balance sheet.

2. A healthy ratio should exist between collateralized and uncollateralized loans. Ask for details as to how the collateralized loans are in fact collateralized, to be sure there is no "window dressing" in the balance sheet.

3. Some banks have borrowed short-term funds and loaned out long-term money to their clients. This is a potentially troublesome situation and it would be revealed if the amounts due from clients appeared as a long-term item on the asset side of the balance sheet, and the amounts on the liability side showed

---

currency control and applies only to new deposits.

only funds due to banks and to clients either at-sight or within a relatively short period.

Swiss Banks and Gold

We have already pointed out that although the United States is emerging as the principal center for the trading of gold futures, the chief market for day-to-day trading in "spot" gold will remain in Europe.

London gained its top position as a trading center for gold in part because of its situation as a seaport, able to receive waterborne shipments of bullion with high efficiency and low security risk. But now, much of South Africa's output of gold is shipped by air; South African Airways and Swiss Air are brisk competitors for this business, and Zurich, with its worldwide financial and banking connections, is rising to challenge London.

The sheer volume of South Africa's shipments requires that its gold be sold in a major world market. Leading London gold dealers (such as Mocatta & Goldsmid, Sharps Pixley, and Samuel Montagu) have been in this business for well over a century. Experience helps, because the bullion business requires skill, not only in shipping but in weighing, assaying, and insuring.

Consider for a moment the scandalous situation that exists at New York's Kennedy Airport, where theft and pilferage are a way of life! That should convince anyone that the world's gold-trading center will remain in Europe for the foreseeable future. Zurich will remain the chief monetary center for gold. Zurich offers the complete anonymity and freedom from regulation that is characteristic of Switzerland and that no other gold-trading center offers.

In addition to being simpler, it should be just as cheap to buy gold in Zurich as anywhere else because of the long familiarity of Swiss banks and bullion dealers in trading the metal.

Remember, too, that the Zurich market is a free auction market that is open all day. The London market, though excellent in many respects, is somewhat unique in that "fixing" of prices takes place only twice a day. Many people expect to buy gold at the last fixed price, but actually it can change in minutes after the fixing. After fixing, London is an auction market.

Furthermore, foreign exchange trading, arbitrage transactions, and other financial dealings that have a relationship to gold all can be carried out in Zurich with expertise for which the Swiss are famous.

And not to be overlooked is another fact: in Switzerland, there is no capital gains levy on profits from gold holdings that may be realized by non-residents.

The fact is that a big trader in gold—a foreign potentate or Arab oil prince—will prefer to keep his gold with a Swiss bank rather than with a highly regarded American banking institution. Other investors, surveying the possibilities that are available, may also come to the conclusion that Switzerland is not only a natural haven for "smart money" but also a logical trading market for gold transactions.

Generally speaking, the small investor in physical bullion may feel more comfortable with an American brokerage firm, while the more sophisticated and affluent type of investor, desiring both safety and secrecy, may prefer to tap the rich lode of expertise in gold and related areas of money management that is traditional among Swiss bankers. The speculator may still prefer to deal in the U.S. futures market.

How a Swiss Bank Handles Gold Orders

For those interested in the details of how Swiss institutions handle gold orders, this is the chronology of such transactions:

Gold orders are received by a Swiss bank by letter, cable, or telephone. As soon as the order arrives, the bank contacts the Zurich gold pool or a London bullion dealer and proceeds to purchase the gold for the client. Orders are executed immediately or, if received during the night, are executed at the opening in the morning.

Gold bars of varying sizes are available, but for investment purposes the standard 12.5-kilogram bar is the most suitable one. (While it is possible to purchase bars of small size—subject to a minimum order of ten ounces—they are proportionately more expensive due to higher manufacturing costs.)

The gold is stored by the bank for its clients and is segregated from the bank's assets. Therefore, should a bank fail, the gold holdings cannot be touched.

As soon as the purchase has been made, a confirmation is sent to the client; his account is charged with the total amount of the purchase and his custodial account is credited with the respective quantity of gold.

Gold Production 1974–78, Non-Communist World
(in metric tons)

	1974	1975	1976	1977	1978
South Africa	758.6	713.4	713.4	699.9	706.4
Canada	52.2	51.4	52.4	54.0	52.9
USA	35.1	32.4	32.2	32.0	30.2
Other Africa:					
Rhodesia	18.6	18.6	17.1	20.0	17.0
Ghana	19.1	16.3	16.6	16.9	14.2
Zaire	4.4	3.6	4.0	3.0	1.0
Other	1.0	1.0	1.0	1.0	1.0
Total Other Africa	43.1	39.5	38.7	40.9	33.2
Latin America:					
Brazil	13.8	12.5	11.6	12.9	13.0
Dominican Rep.	—	3.0	12.7	10.7	10.8
Colombia	8.2	10.8	10.3	9.2	9.0
Mexico	3.9	4.7	5.4	6.7	6.2
Peru	2.7	2.9	3.0	3.4	3.7
Nicaragua	2.4	1.9	2.0	2.0	2.3
Other	5.9	6.0	8.0	8.0	8.5
Total Lat. America	36.9	41.8	53.0	52.9	53.5
Asia:					
Philippines	17.3	16.1	16.3	19.4	20.2
Japan	5.5	4.7	4.0	4.6	6.1
India	3.2	3.0	3.3	2.9	2.8
Other	2.7	2.7	3.0	3.0	3.0
Total Asia	28.7	26.5	26.6	29.9	32.1
Europe	11.6	11.0	11.4	13.2	12.5
Oceania:					
Papua/New Guinea	20.5	17.9	20.5	22.3	23.4
Australia	16.2	16.3	15.4	19.2	20.2
Other	3.2	3.2	3.0	4.0	4.7
Total Oceania	39.9	37.4	38.9	45.5	48.3
Non-Communist World Total	1006.1	953.4	966.6	968.3	969.1

Source: Reprinted by permission of Consolidated Gold Fields.

If a client wishes to sell the gold, he follows a similar procedure: namely, instructing the bank by letter, phone, or cable.
The bank again approaches the Zurich gold pool and sells the
indicated quantity. Once a sale has taken place, the account is
credited with the amount of the proceeds of the sale, and the
custodial account is charged with the respective number of
ounces of gold that have been sold.

Gold futures contracts (see Chapter 5), both long and short,
can also be arranged. The minimum contract size is fifty kilo-
grams.

A cash margin deposit amounting to 50 percent of the total
contract amount is required; the 50 percent must be deposited
in cash and will be credited to a non-interest-bearing margin
account. The margin must be maintained during the period of
the contract, and the bank is entitled to call for additional margin should it become necessary.

The mechanics for gold futures are the same as for spot purchases and sales, the only difference being the price; on a purchase the client would pay a premium for the futures price and
on a sale he would also receive the premium. Premiums vary
according to market conditions, but in general they are based
on the Eurodollar rate.

For each purchase of a futures contract, the bank issues a
confirmation including the due date of the contract. On the due
date the contract is automatically closed out and settlement
takes place on that day. However, contracts can be closed before the due date, or they can be "rolled over" on the due date.

The basic difference between the outright purchase of gold
bullion and a forward contract in gold is this: when the
gold bullion is bought, the client is the owner of the metal; in
a gold futures transaction, the client only has a claim against
a gold account.

Canadian Banks

Canada is the second-largest gold producer (after South
Africa) in the non-Communist world, and historically Canadian banks have played a well-defined role in satisfying the
demand for gold from Canadian citizens and from others at-
tracted to the yellow metal. Unlike the U.S., Canada has never
prohibited the private ownership of gold.

During the forty-year period when American private citizens

were legally prohibited from owning gold, Canadian banks were in the uncomfortable position, usually, of having to reject Americans wishing to buy gold, while serving the needs and desires of Canadians and other non-Americans. Most Canadian banks simply refused to sell gold to customers who gave an American address, but as a rule bank officers did not insist on examining the passports of potential customers.

Thus it is difficult—if not impossible—to estimate with any accuracy the extent of American gold holdings in Canada. The amount is probably substantial, but it is doubtful if it approaches the hoard of the metal believed to be squirreled away in Swiss banks on behalf of U.S. citizens.

Insofar as Canadians are concerned, gold has been legally bought, sold, exported, and imported for years without license or legal restriction in Canada. In this respect the Canadians and Swiss part company with those who consider gold a "barbarous relic." Instead, many Canadians look upon the metal as a stable, internationally accepted form of security and they have accounted for a fairly consistent, though not overwhelming, demand for the metal at the windows of the leading banks of their country. Inquiries about gold have accelerated from time to time when gold fever grips the public.

Now that Americans are no longer barred from gold ownership, the Canadian banks should be in a good position to make sales to U.S. residents. A survey indicates that charges by the Canadian institutions for their services are moderate, and their bookkeeping procedures are uncomplicated.

The Bank of Nova Scotia is Canada's largest gold trader and is probably the single biggest buyer of Canada's gold output, which totaled almost 53 million troy ounces in 1978. Because many of its customers prefer a document attesting to ownership of gold rather than physical possession of the metal, the Bank of Nova Scotia—which sells at some 985 branches throughout the nation—offers gold certificates in multiples of 10 fine ounces, or one kilogram, and traded on the same basis as actual gold. The certificates may be considered as warehouse receipts against unallocated gold. The bank maintains 100 percent coverage in its vaults for all gold for which it has issued certificates.

These well-known gold certificates have come into fairly wide use since the end of World War II, and are redeemable by the issuing bank in Canada. The metal represented by the certificate may be sold at any time and the proceeds transferred into virtually any monetary unit. A transfer of ownership of a certificate also is a relatively simple procedure.

The certificates have been used as collateral for loans and it is possible to purchase them on margin if the buyer is deemed to be credit-worthy. The simplicity of these certificates makes them attractive to buyers who prefer to avoid the cumbersome process of taking physical possession of gold; while at the same time the owner has an instrument that can be used as collateral, sold, or transferred to another owner without difficulty. Of course similar instruments have been developed by American firms, including stock exchange member firms that issue certificates of title to gold.

The Bank of Nova Scotia, with its long history as a gold-trading bank, offers almost a supermarket's selection of gold shapes: tiny wafers weighing 5, 10, 20, or 25 grams; bars of 1, 2, 5, 10, 20, 40, 100, and 400 ounces to bars of one-fourth, one-half, or one full kilo. The bank is also a marketing outlet for the new one-ounce gold Maple Leaf coins, which sell at a premium above spot gold. An Ontario sales tax of 7 percent applies to gold coins on which delivery is taken in the province, but there is no tax on bullion.

The Canadian Imperial Bank of Commerce, which probably ranks second in Canada to the Bank of Nova Scotia as a gold bank, also sells bullion in a variety of sizes and shapes, and selected bullion coins, including the Maple Leaf, Krugerrand, Mexican 50-peso pieces, Austrian 100-corona coins, and Russian chervonetz coins, which contain one-fourth ounce of pure gold. The bank also sells gold certificates in multiples of 10 ounces, and silver certificates in multiples of 100 ounces.

The Royal Bank of Canada, headquartered in Montreal, sells gold and silver in one-kilo bars, and offers gold Maple Leaf coins for sale. Its minimum commission on any sale of coins or bullion is $10.

Chapter 7

Gold Coins: Bullion vs. Numismatic Coins

"Never in the three decades of the International Monetary Fund and the World Bank has inflation posed a more universal threat to the world's economic and social system."

—Hans Apel,
Finance Minister of West Germany

FOR THOUSANDS OF years men have been collecting gold coins. Countless fortunes have been made speculating or investing in coins. Lives have been saved during war when coins have been exchanged for food, or even bartered for a human life.

Small wonder then that the same attraction to coins that prevailed in ancient times persists to this day. Millions of people in all corners of the globe collect coins for esthetic pleasure, as a store of value, as a hedge against the collapse of paper currencies, and as a semipermanent form of investment.

Gold coins, by their very nature, have some fundamental advantages over gold bullion and gold shares: they are easily portable, they can readily be concealed, and they can be purchased and sold without extensive record keeping. They are ideal investments for the small investor, and likewise have a useful role in meeting the needs of large investors. For those who wish to take physical possession of their gold holdings, it makes more sense to do so in the form of coins than bullion.

On the negative side, it must be recognized that coins—like bullion—are non-income-producing investments and therefore must appreciate in order to offset their carrying charges such as insurance, storage, shipping fees, and the like.

It is common knowledge that coins have frequently been used to transfer wealth from one country to another. In some countries they are a popular means of avoiding punitive taxation. We do not recommend them for such purposes, but it is a recognized fact of life that gold coins, in effect, are a private approach to the ownership of gold in many parts of the world.

Bullion-type gold coins tend to move directly with the price of gold bullion. This tendency, it may be noted, is also true of gold shares, but the latter tend to discount market expectations.

U.S. Policy

Minting of gold coins in the United States was halted in 1933, and the Gold Reserve Act of 1934, which prohibited the private ownership of gold, also confiscated all gold coins held by Americans. An exception was made for coins with "recognizable numismatic value."

This was an ambiguous restriction and it was not rigidly enforced by the Treasury. In any event, many coins were retained by their holders and it has been estimated that a substantial volume of these gold coins found their way abroad. (Many have since become collectors' items.)

In 1954 the Treasury declared that all coins minted before 1933 would be presumed to be rare. This action, in effect, legitimized the ownership of gold coins and virtually eliminated the threat of confiscation.

With the legalization of gold ownership, there is no further impediment to purchase of all types of gold coins, in any amount, regardless of any arbitrary distinction by the Treasury. But it is still worth noting that a prohibition against gold ownership, once lifted, can be reinstated again at some future time. Congress, it may be recalled, has traditionally been ambivalent on the subject, often expressing opinions but usually leaving the final decision up to the President. If history repeats itself and a prohibition against gold ownership is reinstated, we have no doubt that large numbers of coins would be retained by their owners. It would be far more difficult for an owner of bullion to resist such a ban. While the threat of government confiscation of gold bullion has historical precedent, it is extremely unlikely that numismatic gold coins would be confiscated. Indeed, should confiscation become a reality, the demand for rare U.S. gold coins may well skyrocket.

Fundamentally, gold coins may be divided into two basic categories:

1. Rare or numismatic coins that derive much of their value from their scarcity and are thus sought by collectors. Prices of such coins are far in excess of their intrinsic gold value. Evaluations in the market place, which reflect their scarcity plus the condition of the item, are highly subjective.

2. Bullion or intrinsic coins, though not especially prized for their scarcity, sell at moderate premiums over their gold bullion content. Since a purchaser pays a premium of no more

than 5 to 7 percent over the bullion value, and the coins can be bought and sold in fairly large quantities without disturbing the market, bullion coins are a practical means for the average investor to take a position in gold.

One example of a numismatic gold coin is an uncirculated 1850 $20 gold piece (Double Eagle) of Liberty Head design, a relatively scarce coin. The price history of this item is revealing. It had a catalogue value of $300 back in 1966. By 1979 the catalogue value had leaped to $2,750, and it is probably worth much more today.

This illustrates the extraordinary appreciation potential in carefully selected numismatic coins. For the ten-year period ending June 1, 1979, a survey conducted by Salomon Brothers, a leading Wall Street investment banking house, indicated that the highest compounded annual investment yield was earned by Chinese ceramics at 18 percent, followed by gold at 16.3 percent, rare coins at 15 percent, and stamps at 15 percent. During this ten-year period, however, bonds returned only 6.1 percent and stocks 2.9 percent, while the consumer price index rose at an annual rate of 6.1 percent.

Such coins, of course, are not easily acquired. As Dr. Joseph de Marinis of Sidemco Coins & Currency, Inc., points out, "It could readily take a full month to purchase just ten choice brilliant uncirculated Barber Half Dollars, 1892–1916, at a reasonable price. Further, the acquisition of ten choice lower mintage dates in the Barber Half Dollar Series at reasonable prices would probably involve a three- to six-month search."

By way of contrast, de Marinis notes, it would probably be possible to confirm an order for up to 1,000 pieces of common coins like the South African Krugerrand at the daily market quotation within minutes.

There is no doubt that over the past few decades, numismatic-type coins, one of the better investment vehicles, have enjoyed a significantly higher degree of appreciation than the more conventional bullion-type coins that are acquired largely for their metallic value, and it may be anticipated that the investor with ample capital and patience will, with proper guidance, uncover further opportunities for long-term enhancement in the numismatic group. Coin expert de Marinis observes that, "Even when common gold and silver coins have appreciated in value, numismatic coins have done better at the very same time. The sum of $50,000 that may be allocated to rare coins in a $1 million portfolio will have more impact on rare coin prices than the remaining $950,000 will have on common coin prices."

Tangible assets such as gold, silver, and rare coins will continue to rise in value as an investment and store of value, hedges against inflation and currency devaluation, a refuge for wealth, and esthetically, a treasure of antiquity. Two economic factors have caused the continuous growth pattern in rare coins: a virtually static supply of any given coin, and an increase in the numbers of collectors and investors. Rare coins offer a high degree of liquidity, privacy, portability, and long-term potential for profitability. Therefore, we believe that tangible assets in the form of gold, silver, and rare coins are to be considered financial assets and one of the most attractive investment vehicles.

In general we feel that the art of selecting numismatic coins is a fascinating and potentially lucrative pursuit and we commend it as part of one's total diversified investment portfolio for longer-term capital appreciation.[1]

However, bullion-type coins, which we strongly recommend as currency insurance and protection for the average person against inflation and currency debasement, sell at modest to occasionally hefty premiums over their bullion content. The following half-dozen are popularly traded bullion coins with which investors would do well to familiarize themselves.

Austrian or Hungarian 100-Corona

These coins contain .9802 troy ounces of gold and are sold at 2 to 4 percent over bullion value. These are presently the lowest-priced gold coins in terms of premium above actual gold content.

The 1908 Hungarian 100-Korona and the 1915 Austrian 100-Corona are being restruck by their respective mints and are available in virtually unlimited quantities. The Austrian coin

---

[1]For those who wish to delve deeper into the subject of coins we recommend:
   High Profits from Rare Coin Investment, Q. David Bowers (Bowers and Ruddy Galleries, Inc., Los Angeles, Calif. 90028)
   Golden Profits from Olden Coins, Ira U. Cobleigh (Goldfax Inc., 25 Park Place, N.Y., N.Y. 10007, $3.70)
   Dr. de Marinis' comments on the coin market place are carried in the weekly advisory letter published by James Sinclair & Company, 90 Broad Street, New York, N.Y. 10004.

has proved a bit more popular in appearance but there is no problem in disposing of lots of 100, 500, or even 1,000 coins within an hour at the prevailing bid price or slightly below. Swiss banks are generally ready to buy lots of 5,000 coins, although this transaction might take several hours to complete. One could probably realize a better rate by selling in smaller lots to different dealers, which is what a Swiss bank would do unless the coins were needed to fill an order.

Mexican 50-Peso

Considered by many to be more popular and attractive than the restrikes mentioned above, the 1947 Mexican 50-Peso is available in unlimited quantity. It contains 1.0256 troy ounces of gold and sells for 5 percent to 10 percent over bullion. Collectors and investors have shown increased interest in the dates that are not being reissued, notably those in the 1920s that sell for about $40 more per coin than the restrikes.

Mexican 50-Peso coins can be bought or sold in quantity as easily as the Austrian and Hungarian coins. The smaller investor should keep in mind, however, that not all dealers will make firm commitments to buy or sell 100-coin lots without a deposit or without first taking possession of the coins.

U.S. $20 Gold Double Eagles

Of the two types of U.S. $20 gold pieces (struck from 1850 to 1933), the "St. Gaudens" design is the more popular. They should be purchased in strictly uncirculated condition although, due to being handled in bags, even mint-state coins will show many scratches or "bag marks" from contact with other coins.

The U.S. Double Eagle contains .97 troy ounces of gold and because of its scarcity sells for a sizable premium, at times 60 to 80 percent, over bullion value. Double Eagles get strong when gold is strong, but also get weak when gold softens, so they are more difficult to trade in a fluctuating bullion market. Also there is not as exact a bid for these coins as for bullion restrikes, nor is there always an eagerness to purchase at the bid price in lots larger than 20 or 50. However, the U.S. $20 gold pieces are getting scarcer as the supply lessens and the coins are held in strong hands. Note that they are not restrikes and can no longer be minted or added to the market.

British Sovereign

Containing just under a quarter-ounce of gold, the British Gold Sovereign continues to be a popular bullion coin in Europe and Great Britain.

Sovereigns have not been minted since 1931. The so-called "new" Sovereigns (Queen Elizabeth type) found their place in the American market but they are considered collectors' items and usually command an extra premium. One would have no trouble selling a lot of 100 or 500 Sovereigns, but there might be some resistance at the 1,000 level and a seller would probably have to settle for a discounted bid at the 5,000- or 10,000-piece level.

South African Krugerrand

This is a newly minted coin that has exactly one troy ounce of gold. Krugerrands were first struck in 1967, but only coins struck as proofs would be considered collectibles. The main interest in the Kruger is that it has exactly one troy ounce of gold and many people (not to mention the South African government) are attempting to promote the coin as "real spending money."

The South African Krugerrand is by far the most popular bullion-type gold coin on the market today, for two reasons. The gold content is exactly one troy ounce, and the premium above the gold bullion price is low, varying from 3 to 5 percent. Instant markets are available worldwide.

Canadian Maple Leaf

Canada has minted a new one-ounce gold coin called the Maple Leaf. It carries a face value of $50, contains one full ounce of gold, and at a current premium of 10 to 12 percent above the bullion gold price, costs $15 to $20 more than the one-ounce Krugerrand. About 1,000,000 coins have been minted. At present it is not a numismatic coin because the mintage is high for one year. If the Maple Leaf traded at the same price as the Krugerrand, it would be a good bullion-type coin to add to one's portfolio.

Recommended Policy Toward Coins

It is our general belief that approximately 10 to 15 percent of an individual's total portfolio should be held in coins. In special circumstances the percentage might be higher. A wealthy individual who is not dependent on income and is primarily interested in the possibility of appreciation in coin investments might conceivably raise this ratio to around 25 percent, carrying 10 to 15 percent of his portfolio in numismatic (rare) coins for capital appreciation.

Let us examine the performance of rare coins, past, present, and future. Let us also view this performance in the face of the present highly volatile precious metals market. How impervious are rare coins to a serious decline in the price of gold? How are they performing in the present recessionary climate? Let us gain a perspective by establishing a parallel between today's volatility and that which occurred in August 1976, when gold dropped to a low of 103. Rare coins, especially silver coins, continued to appreciate at the same escalating pace, while rare gold coins continued upward moderately. With the volatility of gold, the appreciation of rare coins is such that they are performing as if gold remained stable or declined sharply.

At the 1979 American Numismatic Association convention, virtually every major dealer had his best show ever. The tone was set on the Thursday prior to official opening of the bourse floor. The extremely rare 1787 Brasher Doubloon, a colonial gold coin and one of only seven known, was hammered down at public auction for $430,000. This was nearly double the record price set a few months back when the 1907 Ultra High Relief $20 gold piece sold for $225,000.

As the price of gold dropped $25 in August 1979, gold coins grew even stronger. One incident immediately comes to mind. A common-date Liberty $5 gold piece in MS-69 condition was purchased by one dealer for $1,700. This coin was in turn sold to another dealer for $2,000. The next morning, a third dealer purchased the coin for $2,300. That same common-date Liberty $5 gold piece, worth about $210 in average condition, appreciated 35 percent in two days.

Another noteworthy highlight of the ANA convention was the sale of a complete set of type III gold dollars, which sold for close to $200,000 (redbook value—under $100,000 in uncirculated condition). In fact, over a dozen individual rare coins have sold in excess of $100,000 in the recent past.

Rare coins will undoubtedly continue to perform well despite the current economic scene. Why? An auspicious development has been occurring: a major new buyer has appeared on the scene, namely, the financial establishment. Rare coins are now being included in clients' portfolios in many of the prominent investment houses as they attempt to purchase "tangible assets." The rush of the financial community to catch up with the demand for "tangible assets" is a reflection of the depth of investors' concern with rising inflation and the subsequent erosion and deterioration of all paper-related assets (stocks, bonds, etc.). With the financial community invading the ranks formerly occupied by collectors only, we shall witness the continued rapid growth of a substantial demand in the face of an already limited, fixed supply.

The bullion-type gold coins on which we place emphasis are the Mexican 50-Peso Centenario, the Austrian 100-Corona, the Hungarian 100-Korona, the U.S. $20 Double Eagle, and the British one-pound Sovereign.

We have been favorably disposed toward the South African Krugerrand, a bullion coin with sex appeal. Of course, there are other common gold coins that may be included in a coin portfolio but those mentioned are good representatives of this genre.

In view of the excellent marketability of bullion-type coins, there is no particular benefit to be derived from diversification per se. However, some countries (such as Mexico) offer a wide variety of coins while others may wish to acquire several, rather than one, of the lowest premium common gold coins.

The portfolios outlined below represent the part of one's assets assigned to coins, *not* one's total investments. I am convinced that the current markets are potentially violent; dollar weakness is far from over, merely waiting for its cue to return. Dr. Joseph de Marinis, a partner in James Sinclair & Company, has assisted in the preparation of the following recommendations; these suggestions obviously require tailoring to the goals and plans of a particular investor.

Portfolio No. 1   Capitalization: Modest
                Coins/Specie Bullion $10,000
Bullion gold coins—Krugerrands, Austrian 100-Coronas, Mexi-

can 50-pesos. This is a moderately conservative interest in gold without the risks of shares or the volatile futures market. We recommend you purchase and take delivery of the gold bullion coins carrying the lowest premium above their gold content.

Portfolio No. 2   Capitalization: Medium
   Coins/Specie Gold $12,500 Rare Coin Distribution
   1. Eight-piece U.S. gold type set. The builder set of U.S. gold coins in brilliant uncirculated condition. Can be added to, in order to complete a set of all 12 types of U.S. gold coins.
   2. A selection of better issued commemorative U.S. silver 50-cent pieces, which we believe are undervalued.
      a. Alabama 1921 Commemorative 50 cents. M.S. (Mint State).
      b. California Jubilee 1925 M.S. 65 Commemorative 50 cents.
      c. York 1936 Commemorative 50 cents.
   3. Remaining coins should include high-quality uncirculated and proof-type coins in key date issues from a series, e.g.:
      a. 1885 Liberty Nickel M.S. 65.
      b. 1907 Barber Quarter M.S. 67.
      c. 1919-D Mercury Dime M.S. 67.
      d. 1927 Standing Liberty Quarter M.S. 65.
      e. 1938-D Walking Liberty Half Dollar M.S. 67.
      f. 1880-O Morgan Silver Dollar M.S. 65.
      g. 1891-CC Ten Dollar Gold Indian M.S. 65.

Portfolio No. 3   Capitalization: Substantial
   Coins/Specie Gold $25,000 Rare Coin Distribution
   1. 12-piece U.S. gold type set. The complete set of modern U.S. gold coins in brilliant uncirculated condition. The set contains three types of U.S. one-dollar gold pieces, two types of 2-dollar gold, two types of 5-dollar gold, one 3-dollar gold, two types of 10-dollar gold, two types of 20-dollar gold.
   2. A selection of better commemorative silver 50-cents:
      a. 1936 Albany Commemorative 50-cent M.S. 65.
      b. 1936 Lynchburg Commemorative 50-cent M.S. 65.
      c. 1915-S Pan-Pacific Commemorative 50-cent M.S. 65.
      d. 1928 Hawaiian Commemorative M.S. 65.

e. 1921 Missouri Commemorative 50-cent M.S. 65.
f. 1936 Norfolk Commemorative 50-cent M.S. 65.
3. A selection of high-quality-type coins in key date issues.
a. 1883 No Cents Liberty Nickel Proof 67.
b. 1911-S Barber Dime M.S. 67.
c. 1909-D Barber Quarter M.S. 65.
d. 1874 Seated Quarter with Arrows Proof 67.
e. 1917 Walking Liberty 50-cent M.S. 65.
f. 1885-S Morgan Silver Dollar M.S. 65.
g. 1886-S Five-Dollar Liberty Gold M.S. 65.
h. 1892-CC Ten-Dollar Gold M.S. 65.

The rationale behind these recommendations is simple. Quality rare coins have continued to appreciate for the past twenty years or longer at a rate of approximately 30 percent a year. Although past performance is no guarantee of future appreciation, we believe that with the addition of investor interest to a market formerly limited to collectors only, rare coins should continue to climb in price because of the dwindling supply. Therefore, we recommend placing a portion of ones portfolio in tangibles, including rare coins, for longer-term capital appreciation.

Coin-Collecting Techniques

Collecting coins differs in a number of fundamental respects from purchasing gold mining shares, gold bullion, or gold futures. In buying stocks, for example, the individual is usually doing business with a member of a major stock exchange or an over-the-counter house and the quotation he obtains on a security issue probably won't differ greatly from one broker to another. (Possible exception: in the over-the-counter market some brokers frequently provide better quotations, as well as execution of orders, than others.)

But unlike the stock brokerage business, the coin business is largely unregulated. There are, at the very least, several hundred important coin dealers in the United States, and the total number, including the one-man shops and fledgling firms, may well run to several thousand.

Thus, in purchasing or selling coins, it is advisable to do business with a reputable concern such as a bank, foreign exchange dealer, member of a recognized securities exchange, or a coin dealer who has been in business for some time and is a well-situated member of his financial community. If the dealer is a member of a recognized professional organization (such as the American Numismatics Association, the International Association of Professional Numismatists, or the Professional Numismatists' Guild), so much the better.

Even if the individual has no doubts about the financial standing of the dealer, he should not hesitate to compare prices from several different sources—he might well wind up saving himself a fair amount of money.

It is well known that the number of coin dealers has proliferated in recent years, together with the mounting interest in investing in coins. While most dealers are respectable businessmen, some have been known to engage in practices that are either illegal or unethical.

It is not unusual, for instance, to pass off "restrikes" as originals. (Restrikes are coins minted from dies of earlier years.) More serious is the risk of counterfeits being passed off as genuine. Counterfeits are a fact of life in the coin business; in Europe there are even quoted markets for both real and counterfeit sovereigns! However, it is possible to minimize this hazard by following a simple practice: when you buy coins, ask for a guarantee of authenticity, *in writing,* from the dealer. If he is a legitimate operator, he will be only too happy to comply.

A Texas court, in a well-publicized case, enjoined one of the leading coin merchants from dealing in margin account contracts for the sale of gold and silver coins. It was alleged that a mere 3 percent of the margin account contracts held by the firm were actually backed or hedged by bags of coins; and while all margin account contracts of the firm were charged high rates of interest, it was alleged by the court that no loan identifiable with any investor could be segregated.

We recommend that the investor avoid dealing in any forward coin contract except in cases where he is thoroughly acquainted with what he is doing, and even then is conducting his business through a reputable bank or a member of an established commodity or securities exchange.

These are some additional points for the would-be coin investor:

• Acquire your coin portfolio carefully over a reasonable period of time rather than in a hasty, undisciplined manner.

• Be especially wary of "bait" advertising by dealers offering "fantastic bargains" or urging you to rush in to buy before it is too late.

• Give preference to uncirculated coins over worn coins, even though this may entail a modest premium. Quality is a significant factor in establishing the value of a coin.

• Beware not only of unscrupulous dealers but also of those who are undercapitalized and who enter the field to make a "fast buck." They may wind up in financial difficulties, unable to serve their customers.

• Be wary of high-powered ads offering gold and silver medals as investments. The medallion mania has reached absurd proportions and medals are being struck to commemorate the most trivial events. If you collect medals as a hobby, fine. But don't buy them for investment purposes, because you may find them difficult or impossible to sell.

• Look out for treated or processed coins that are offered as uncirculated or "proof" items when buying numismatic coins. Also, diversify your holdings in this category—you may find that it is better to hold a reasonably wide variety of numismatic coins rather than one or two items of exceptionally high value.

• Remember that a coin collector faces a number of hazards, including counterfeiting, theft, and wear. Coins, therefore, should be kept in a safe place such as a private depository.

• Above all, seek out expert advice and look out for charlatans, especially if you are dabbling in the coin field for the first time.

Criteria for Selection of Rare Coins

1. High quality.
2. Diversification among low, medium, and high priced coins.
3. Price range.
   Coin prices are *not* the result of
   a) age, b) sentiment, or c) the price you paid.
   Coin prices *are* the result of
   a) demand, b) condition, and c) mintage.
4. Collector stimulus.
5. Liquidity.
6. Potential for appreciation.

Criteria for Selection of an Adviser

1. Seek an adviser whose sole and primary objective is providing expert advice in the field of numismatics.
2. Seek an adviser who specializes in the acquisition of high-quality coins.
3. Seek an adviser who is interested in dealing with a select group of investors whose collections he can continually monitor, appraise, and develop.
4. Seek an adviser who will aid in disposal of your collection.
5. Seek an adviser who is compatible with your goals and personal requirements.
6. Seek an adviser from referrals of other investors as to his performance, integrity, and reliability.
7. Seek an adviser who is involved in the numismatic community, e.g., a life member of ANA, the American Numismatic Society, or other recognized numismatic organization.

The performance of both bullion-type coins and numismatic (rare) coins speaks for itself as an outstanding adjunct to ones investment portfolio. Prudence and personal circumstances will dictate what is best for you.

Chapter 8

South African
Gold Shares*

"Gold is still our most important mineral and South Africa today produces about 78% of the total gold production of the Free World. Apart from gold, however, South Africa has been endowed with a wide variety of other minerals, including several of strategic importance."

—Hon. Gerald Browne,
Secretary for the Dept. of Finance,
Republic of South Africa

---

*Information in this chapter was largely assembled by John Crowley, a specialist in gold mining shares and a partner of James Sinclair and Company.

SOUTH AFRICAN GOLD shares have always possessed a degree of sensitivity to the price performance of gold bullion. The connection is clear. The investor reasons correctly enough that high gold prices will be reflected in higher earnings and dividends by the mines, assuming consistent production schedules.

There are more than fifty South African gold issues worthy of the investor's attention. These "Kaffirs" fall into three general classes: high-quality shares, medium-quality shares, and leveraged shares. In categorizing Kaffirs or any other precious metal mining shares for a portfolio, one must take these criteria into account:

1. Proven ore reserves.

2. Grade recovery, that is, the approximate number of grams of gold that can be recovered from each ton of ore milled, on an annualized basis.

3. Financial condition of the mine, given that the mine has proven ore reserves and established recovery rates. With this data, the mine directors can establish a production schedule, based on projected working costs, projected capital expenditures long and short term, available financing, and projected market behavior for gold bullion. This projection may be based on Chamber of Mines estimates of sales potential, demand from industrial and investment outlets, and international events that affect bullion prices. A mine's production schedule is determined mainly by the mine's cost per ounce of production.

4. Other important by-products of the mine in South Africa. This usually refers to uranium, a significant by-product of gold mining. South Africa produces an estimated 13 percent of the Free World's uranium.

5. Yield, that is, the rate of return to the investor on an annualized basis. The South African gold shares pay the highest yields of any equity group, most of them presently paying 14 percent or more based on share prices at the time of the declaration of dividends.

Quality shares generally represent mines that have large ore reserves, high grade recovery (10 grams of gold per ton, or better, on an annualized basis), a recovery cost of $150 per ounce or less, some uranium production, and a yield of 14 percent or more on the market price.

Medium-quality shares will possess some but not all of these characteristics. Leveraged shares are probably the most interesting of all the South African gold shares because they are more sensitive to price fluctuations of bullion. These mines usually operate from marginal grade ore, increase their production when bullion prices rise, and show high profits on high gold prices. As a rule, leveraged mines have low proven ore reserves, recovery rates averaging less than 8 grams per ton of ore, and relatively high-cost production, in the range above $150 an ounce. Only some of these mines co-produce uranium. The most interesting feature of these mines is the higher yields they offer, a trade-off for the slightly higher risk the investor assumes in buying these shares. Just as these mines adjust production schedules on a shorter-term basis, market psychology creates more volatile activity, their share prices sometimes lead bullion price movements, and at all times they are sensitive to such movements.

The South African gold shares have a wide international following. They are traded on ten major international markets, the most active being London, Johannesburg, and New York. Until recently, most of the share trading came from Johannesburg, near which some of the mines are located, and London. The U.S., however, has become a major source of share demand, and over-the-counter market makers compete vigorously for a major share of market activity.

The Kaffirs are traded internationally on over-the-counter markets in the U.S. and also are traded very actively by "jobbers" or market makers on the London and Johannesburg stock exchanges.

South African law bars the transfer of voting power in South African mining companies outside of South Africa, so investors elsewhere receive depository receipts rather than voting shares. These depository receipts are issued by transfer agents in one of the three cities where Kaffirs are traded: Johannesburg, London, or New York. When dividends are declared, the transfer agent in New York remits payment to the owners of record in U.S. dollars; the London agent pays in pounds sterling; and the South African–based agent pays in Rands.

The international investor (the non–South African) may buy participation through the London, New York, and Johannesburg registries. Voting shares may be bought only through members of the Johannesburg Stock Exchange and must be held in South Africa.

The main advantage in owning a particular registry is the matter of location. Many international banks, especially those in Switzerland, prefer to buy shares registered in London or Johannesburg because of their easy access to those centers and their close ties to the London transfer agents. Some institutions even in the U.S. prefer to register their ADRs (American Depository Receipts) overseas in order to maintain the assets outside U.S. jurisdiction. This seems an unnecessary precaution. The chance that the U.S. government will confiscate such securities is extremely remote. If the U.S. should decide to discourage overseas investment in order to encourage retention of capital in the U.S., the simplest device would be to raise the interest equalization tax—a tax levied on U.S. ownership of foreign corporations—from its present level of zero to something like 10 percent. This would automatically make the shares more expensive to the U.S. share buyer or, in effect, make the shares more valuable to the U.S. shareholder.

The international market makers carry their share inventories in the three main registries. Actually there is a fourth registry, International Depository Receipts (IDRs), which can be registered either in New York, London, or Brussels. This is a bearer certificate, in which only the certificate number and the number of shares are recorded by the transfer agent. It is the responsibility of the bearer to clip coupons attached to the receipts and redeem them for dividends through the collection agent. The disadvantage of this form of registry is that the transfer into or out of this form takes several weeks. Most brokers do not carry inventories of IDRs. The holder of an IDR wishing to sell his shares must first transfer them into another registry.

The Ex-Dollar Premium and the Security Rand

Because the market for Kaffirs is widely based among international investors, currency considerations on the purchase and sale of the shares become a matter of some concern. Shares purchased by residents of the United Kingdom were made subject to an "Ex-dollar premium," a premium added to the value of shares traded in London. The premium was a device to discourage demand for foreign registered shares, and could be increased or reduced to zero through action by Parliament.

In times when the premium is in effect, it increases the cost of all international shares, including Kaffirs. The effect may be to create additional share liquidity or create additional demand. If the pound is under selling pressure, the government may increase the Ex-dollar premium, discouraging U.K. demand for foreign shares by making shares purchased in the U.K. slightly more expensive. This may also encourage U.K. holders to sell, and these shares may find their way to the New York or Johannesburg markets.

When the strength of the pound leads to a reduction in the Ex-dollar premium, however, additional buying may arise from U.K. investors. This in fact did occur on October 23, 1979, when the Ex-dollar premium was dropped to zero percent.

South Africa has set up regulations designed to attract foreign investment in South African shares. Such an investor, wishing to buy shares in the South African market, may do so —subject to approval of the Reserve Bank of South Africa— with "Security Rands" or "Financial Rands," which are available at a discount of approximately 20 percent. The foreign investor reaps the benefits of this privilege on the sale of his securities. If he agrees to sell his holdings to another foreign investor in South Africa, his investment is liquidated into "official" Rands at a rate of 1.2080 and converted to a currency of his choice, including, of course, U.S. dollars if he wishes. This gives him a built-in profit of about 20 percent on his original investment—based on the fact that he received approval to buy "Security Rands"—plus or minus whatever fluctation has occurred in the value of the shares.

In December 1978, the DeKock Commission recommended that the Pretoria government relax its restrictions on the foreign purchase of Security Rands and allow the discounted Rand to be used in other areas of capital investment in South Africa. It was reasoned that this would encourage economic development, to the benefit of both black and white residents of South Africa. In fact, the program was instituted to promote private real estate ownership for blacks.

The Kaffir market in South Africa would be affected by fluctuations of the Security Rand. If demand increased for the Security Rand because of foreign demand for South African stocks, this would reduce the discount and eventually narrow the advantage accorded to buyers of Security Rands.

Eventually, the point would arrive when foreign demand for the Security Rand became so high that irregular liquidation of shares in Johannesburg would create liquidity in London and New York markets. If the South African government finds that demand for the Security Rand is creating unusual pressure on the equity markets, it can instruct the South African Reserve Bank to supply additional Security Rands to foreigners to limit the pressure on share prices. The U.S. market for Kaffirs can be affected if the Interest Equalization Tax should be raised above its current level of zero.

The South African Investment Climate

The industrial potential of South Africa ranks it high among the industrialized nations such as the U.S., West Germany, Great Britain, France, and Japan. Yet South Africa must deal with a very sensitive political, social, and economic climate involving its race relations, which has deterred some investors from placing their capital in South African investments.

It is important to note that the South African economy is heavily dependent on mining, and that the Western world, in turn, depends upon South Africa for a broad array of strategic materials. South Africa produces 72 percent of the Free World's gold and 11 percent of its uranium, and its above-ground stockpile of uranium represents about 18 percent of the Free World's total. South Africa's growing industrial development, however, has diminished the relative importance of gold mining; gold production now represents 8.5 percent of its GNP, vs. 15 percent as recently as 1976–78. Political and social changes are inevitable in South Africa, and there are growing indications that the nation is initiating change within the country to improve the economic and social conditions of its black majority.

Social and political growth move slowly, and South Africa has demonstrated tremendous initiative in this area, courageously so for a country just recovering from a severe economic slump. In January 1979, the South African government adopted a number of economic reforms proposed by the DeKock Commission. The effect of these changes will be to unpeg the Rand from the U.S. dollar; for a time the South African Reserve Bank will be empowered to intervene, but this power will be phased out with the effect that the Rand will be allowed gradually to find its own level. The Security Rand will be allowed to trade with fewer restrictions on its purchase by foreigners. The ultimate aim of these reforms is to encourage foreign speculation in the Rand on a cash and forward basis with a minimum of Reserve Bank intervention, in the hope of eventually abolishing the two-tier exchange rate system.

In May 1979, Labor Minister Stephanus P. Botha agreed to adopt the principles of the Wiehahn Commission for the promotion of greater job mobility for black workers, thus helping to solve problems arising from a shortage of skilled white labor. "Job reservation" would cease. The commission described its objective as opening a channel for the realization of black aspirations.

We feel that South Africa's economic growth mandates greater participation for all; it seems to us this will promote greater labor efficiency and give the urban black workers a more permanent stake in their jobs and in the nation's economic future.

In addition, South Africa has taken a major step toward achieving energy self-sufficiency. Its massive Sasol I and Sasol II plants will convert South Africa's abundant coal into liquid fuel and natural gas. The Sasol project has already made South Africa 70 percent self-sufficient in energy; total self-sufficiency is the goal set for 1984.

The Union Corporation Mine is developing a method of mining called carbon pulping, which, when perfected, is expected to lower costs and increase recovery in gold mining for a substantial gain in mining efficiency.

Though there are still problems to be resolved in Namibia and South West Africa and with Zimbabwe-Rhodesia, some of these are moving closer to solution. Great Britain's initiative in attempting to solve the Rhodesian question has met with some encouraging success. The United Nations is attempting to develop an internationally acceptable settlement to the question of Namibian autonomy. The international concern with these matters is a measure of South Africa's importance to the Western world.

Nevertheless, an investor must realize that the political and social climate of Southern Africa can affect the psychology and the behavior of the markets. The prudent investor will take these factors into account in deciding how much of his resources he wishes to commit to this type of investment.

The Shares

There are three types of mining issues that can generally be described as South African gold share investments.

The finance house invests directly in mining companies in order to participate in the planning of mining operations and to share in the companies' profits. A finance house backs mining operations with substantial capital in order to develop operating mines or establish new mining properties with the hope of establishing production at some date in the future. The finance house also invests in insurance companies, which provide capital for mining ventures in diamonds, iron, and coal.

Holding companies are favored for the purpose of developing income through equity earnings, specifically through the capital appreciation of shares in individual mines in the companies' portfolios.

Individual mining companies issue shares that are traded by professional traders and individual investors, as well as by finance houses, holding companies, and mutual funds. The public can also buy shares in the finance houses, holding companies, and the mutual funds.

Several mutual funds are currently investing in South African as well as North American shares. Two that we would recommend are International Investors Inc., an open-end mutual fund based in New York, and the United Services Fund, a no-load gold fund based in Dallas, Texas.

The two major holding companies formed for investment in South African gold mining shares are:

ASA Ltd.
Listing: New York Stock Exchange
Shares outstanding: 9,600,000
Fiscal year ends Nov. 30.
ASA deals specifically with shares quoted on the Johannesburg exchange, yet is not quoted on the JSE, and its shares cannot be owned by South African residents. The company is obligated by its charter to invest 50% or more of its assets in South African gold shares. Its total investment must be com-

mitted to South African assets, but this may include cash and South African government securities. ASA may not commit more than 20% of its assets into any one issue.

ASA's market value tends to lag its net asset value. This is attributable to the fact that it offers the same degree of risk that all South African gold shares offer, yet produces a lower yield. The individual mines in ASA's portfolio offer higher yield and the same risk; what ASA offers is a degree of diversification among the mining companies. Individuals or finance houses choosing to invest directly in the mines may do so.

Anglo American Gold Investment Co. (Amgold)
   Listing: Over the Counter—NASDAQ
   Shares outstanding: 21,952,012
   Fiscal year ends Feb. 28.
   Amgold offers the same yield to the investor as do the individual mines, about 16%. The market has shown much interest in Amgold in late 1978 and 1979, sending its shares from a low of 18⅝ to a late 1979 high of 59½. With the addition of Deelkraal to its portfolio in late 1978, Amgold holds shares in most of the widely followed gold mining companies.

The Finance Houses

Anglo American Corp. of South Africa Ltd. (Anglys)
   Listing: OTC—NASDAQ
   Shares outstanding: 222,850,030
   Fiscal year ends March 31.
   This house represents one of the world's largest mining interests with investments not only in gold and gold mining but with a 30% stake in DeBeers (diamonds); 36% of Charter Consolidated, a finance house; 48% of Amgold, 41% of Johannesburg Consolidated Investment (another finance house) and 49% of Amcoal (a major coal producer.)
   Anglys was responsible for 37% of South Africa's gold production, 44% of its uranium output, and 33% of its coal production. Anglys' copper mines in Zambia and Canada made the house responsible for 12% of world production of copper. This is truly one of the giants of the industry.

Anglo-Transvaal Consolidated Investment Company Ltd. (Anglovaal)

Listing: OTC
Shares outstanding: 3,566,000 common; 2,873,500 preferred
Financial year ends June 30.
This finance house over the last few years has emphasized its commitment to industrial metals, such as Associated Manganese, which accounted for 33% of the total net assets at valuation. Anglovaal also has Middle Wils and Prieska Copper as subsidiaries.

Barlow Rand Ltd. (Barlows)
Listing: OTC
Shares outstanding: 107,413,569 common; 12,191,634 preferred
Financial year ends September 30.
Barlow is another finance house well diversified in South African industrial situations. Barlow's main interest in mining is through Rand Mines Ltd., wholly owned by Barlow.

Charter Consolidated Ltd. (Charter)
Listing: OTC
Shares outstanding: 104,792,981
Financial year ends March 31.
This diverse mining finance house is one of the real giants in South Africa. It also holds many international investments as well, such as a 49% holding of Minorco, which holds 49% of Zambia Copper. Minorco also has 29% of Engelhard Minerals. Charter owns 24% of Anglo American Corp. of Canada, which owns 38.8% of Hudson Bay Mining. Charter also controls 25.8% of Selection Trust and Rio Tinto Zinc. Its gold holdings consist of 6% of Anglo American Corp. of South Africa.

Consolidated Gold Fields Ltd. (Consolidated)
Listing: OTC
Shares outstanding: 119,808,051.
Financial year ends June 30.
This is one of the world's major mining finance houses; it owns 45.9% of Gold Fields of South Africa, a major gold mining finance house. Consolidated Gold Fields has many interests in industries in the U.K. It is heavily invested in East and West Driesfontein and Kloof, three major gold mines. Consolidated Gold Fields also has major investments in gold, uranium, and tin in Australia.

DeBeers Consolidated Mines
  Listing: OTC-NASDAQ
  Shares outstanding: 359,780,000
  Financial year ends December 31.
  DeBeers is the giant in diamond production, accounting for
the production of 40% of the world's diamonds. DeBeers reported a record breaking year in 1978, with sales of more than
$2.5 billion. Partially responsible was a 17% increase in gem
prices, declared by the Central Selling Organization, the trade's
world regulatory agency governing pricing and distribution.

General Mining and Finance (General Mining)
  Shares outstanding: 42,000,000 common; 250,000 preferred
  Financial year ends Dec. 31.
  General Mining is second in size only to Anglo American
Corp., in financial resources. General Mining controls 48.2% of
Union Corp. It has major holdings in Kinross, Stilfontein, St.
Helena, and Winklehaak, as well as a major position in Buffels-
fontein, all major South African gold mines. General Mining
holds major interests in the Impala, Lydenberg, and Rusten-
berg platinum mining groups and is also a major holder of
Trans Natal Coal, a large South African coal producer. General
Mining is very much involved in other South African industrial
products.

Gold Fields of South Africa Ltd. (Gold Fields)
  Listing: OTC-NASDAQ
  Shares outstanding: 16,211,477
  Financial year ends June 30.
  Gold Fields is considered one of the top mining finance
houses, with substantial commitment to East Driefontein, West
Driefontein, and Kloof. It now holds 50.3% of a new mine called
Deelkraal and has sizable holdings in Blyvoorintzicht, Western
Deep Levels, Libanon, and Elandsrand. Deelkraal and Elands-
rand are two new mines which will be going into full produc-
tion shortly. Gold Fields also has holdings in other major indus-
trial mines, yet 75% of its investment portfolio is in gold mines.
Gold Fields is also developing iron ore mining in Brazil.

Johannesburg Consolidated Investment Co. Ltd. (Johnnies)
  Listing: OTC
  Shares outstanding: 7,105,600 common; 40,000,000 preferred

Financial year ends June 30.

Johnnies is not as heavily involved in gold mining as are the other houses, but it does own 21.6% of Randfontein, a high-quality gold mine, 6% of Elsburg/Western Areas leveraged gold mines, 7.9% of Johnson Matthey, a major London gold broker.

Johnnies' main area of investment is in DeBeers, 6.4%; Rustenberg Platinum, 13.4%; South African Breweries, 16.5%; and it owns 52% of Tavistock, a major South African gold producer.

Union Corporation Ltd. (Union Corp.)
Listing: OTC-NASDAQ
Shares outstanding: 58,100,000
Financial year ends December 31.

Union Corp. is a subsidiary of General Mining and owns 50.9% of General Mining. Union Corp. has 7.9% of its assets in Kinross, 8.4% in St. Helena, 8.5% in Unisel, and 6.9% in Winklehaak. Union Corp. owns 48% of UC Investments, a holding company in South African gold mines. In fact, Union Corp. is currently developing a new gold mine called Beisa Mines Ltd., that will also yield uranium. Union Corp. also owns 53% of a major producer of paper in South Africa.

The Individual Gold Mines

(All listings are OTC, unless marked with*, indicating NASDAQ.)

Afrikander Lease
Shares outstanding: 6,727,500
Fiscal year ends Dec. 30.

This new property, ready for exploitation, will begin production in December 1979, at a rate of about 15,000 tons a month. The ore will be developed and treated by Vaal Reefs, one of South Africa's largest gold mines. This young property, expected to yield low-grade gold ore, along with uranium, could be an interesting long-term situation.

Blyvoorinzicht (Blyvoors)
Shares outstanding: 24,000,000
Fiscal year ends June 30.

Blyvoors can be considered at best a leveraged producer of gold and uranium, with a production cost of $115 per ounce. This mine yields approximately 16% per annum to the investor. At present the mine has a capacity to treat 160,000 tons per month. We expect that grade recovery will fall below its current level of 10 grams per ton, but interest is justified due to its gold-and-uranium consideration.

Bracken
   Shares outstanding: 14,000,000
   Fiscal year ends September 30.
   This highly leveraged mine is very close to cessation of operations underground, a stage known as "breakup." Its output continues to decline while working costs rise sharply. Only high current prices for bullion allow this mine to continue operation. Its current cost of production is $114 per ounce, while its grade recovery is 6.1 grams per ton. We feel it is an interesting play for short-term consideration only in violently positive gold markets.

Buffelsfontein (Buffels)
   Shares outstanding: 11,000,000
   Fiscal year ends June 30.
   This higher quality gold-uranium producer has maintained steady production over the last few years by developing the South River Bulge area, tributed from Vaal Reefs, and by having Stilfontein mill small quantities of ore, as well as using surface stockpiles to keep the mill at full capacity. Buffels is a long-life mine with approximately 16 to 18 years of production remaining, with a cost per ounce of $158 and grade recovery of 8.5 grams per ton. Uranium has become very important to the mine as profits have risen by 50%.

Deelkraal
   Shares outstanding: 99,540,000
   Financial year ends December 31.
   The major shareholders of this mine, Gold Fields of South Africa and Charter Consolidated, have helped finance this mine into production, investing well beyond the original projection of South African Rands 100,000,000; production is scheduled to begin in December 1979. Outside of the principal ore body yields should be low in terms of grade, but the best ore veins should yield 10 grams per ton. This was all according to expectations. Deelkraal could prove to be an interesting long-term play.

Doornefontein (Doorns)
 Shares outstanding: 9,828,000
 Fiscal year ends June 30.
 Doorns can best be described as a marginal producer of short
life expectancy, with more than 10 years of life remaining in
the mine. Grade recovery is currently 8.4 grams per ton at a cost
of $147 per ounce.

Durban Roodepoort Deep Ltd. (Durban Deeps)
 Shares outstanding: 2,325,000
 Financial year ends December 31.
 Durban is a leveraged, short-life mine on heavy state assistance since 1975. Though recent higher levels for gold helped to
improve working profits, a drop in grade recovery to 3.5 grams
per ton at a cost of $242 per ounce did not help matters. The
southwest lease area also turned out to be disappointing. Profits
have improved enough to reinstate dividends, and investors
can now realize 16% annually, making Durban an exciting
short-term play.

East Driefontein Gold Mining Co. Ltd. (East Dries)
 Shares outstanding: 54,510,000
 Financial year ends December 31.
 Though East Dries has a large number of common shares
outstanding, we still consider it one of the outstanding
mines of South Africa, with the lowest production cost at $54
an ounce and the highest grade recovery at 20.1 grams per
ton. It is a long-life mine yielding 16% per annum. We
would recommend this issue highly for long-term consideration.

East Rand Gold and Uranium (ERGO)
 Shares outstanding: 40,000,000
 Financial year ends March 31.
 ERGO is unique in that it is not a mine but a processing plant,
which treats dumps or waste from other mines in the hope of
extracting more gold, more uranium, and more sulfur. This is
done by dumping these wastes into huge dams that are treated
by highly skilled labor. Recovery is marginal, but it is a cheap
operation. The South African government foresees a role for
this type of technology in all other areas of mining. The technique is being used for excess diamond recovery. ERGO has

been in operation only since 1978, but it may have a very bright future.

East Rand Proprietary Mines Ltd. (ERPM)
   Shares outstanding: 3,960,000
   Financial year ends December 31.
   This leveraged mine is comparable to Durban in the sense that high-priced gold makes this situation attractive; however, because of technical considerations, its profits are highly sensitive to gold price fluctuations. Currently, plans have been revived for expansion of the mine, a project made feasible only by high price levels for bullion. ERPM is on heavy state assistance, and with the help of this aid has resumed dividend payments at a rate of 16% to 18% per annum, depending on working profits. We can recommend ERPM for short-term consideration. Grade recovery is 5.0 grams per ton at a cost of $267 per ounce.

Elandsrand
   Shares outstanding: 75,484,238
   Financial year ends December 31.
   Elandsrand went into production in December 1978, well ahead of schedule. Though it is a new mine and recovery is currently at 4.8 grams per ton, it should prove an interesting long-term play.

Free State Geduld Mines Ltd. (Freegulls or FSG)
   Shares outstanding: 10,440,000
   Financial year ends September 30.
   Free State is one of the higher-quality gold mines, with grade recovery at 12.6 grams per ton at a cost of $94 per ounce. It is also involved in Anglo American Corp.'s Joint Metallurgical Scheme, by which several mines work together with special loans granted by Anglo to develop uranium. Free State recently bought Free State Development to help improve production and recovery schedules. Free State has a life expectancy of 16 years. It now yields 16% per annum.

Free State Saaiplaas Gold Mining Co. Ltd. (Saaiplaas or FSS)
   Shares outstanding: 28,100,000
   Financial year ends September 30.
   FSS is a leveraged mine which relies heavily on profits from

uranium sold in the Joint Metallurgical Scheme; it happens to be the major beneficiary of the scheme. Gold production until this year was disappointing, yet the underdeveloped western area may have good potential. Gold recovery at best was 3.4 grams per ton at a cost of $256 per ounce. Recommended for short-term consideration only.

Grootvlei Proprietary Mines Ltd. (Groots)
   Shares outstanding: 11,438,816
   Financial year ends December 31.
   Higher production and slightly better grade recovery of 4.5 grams per ton helped boost the earnings for this leveraged gold producer in 1979. In fact, additional capital expenditures can now be considered in order to prolong the life expectancy of this mine, now estimated at four to five years at best. However, with its high sensitivity to gold price movement and a yield of 25% per annum, Grootvlei deserves consideration.

Harmony Gold Mining Co. Ltd. (Harmony)
   Shares outstanding: 26,884,650
   Financial year ends June 30.
   Harmony, over the last few years, has made a major commitment to uranium development, as demonstrated by construction of an additional plant at the Merriespruit section. Though marginal gold properties purchased in 1974 have just recently shown favorable results, higher gold prices will contribute to working profits, which are jointly recorded with uranium earnings. This method of accounting is done so that when gold grades decline, as they are now doing, uranium will play a greater role as its selling price rises. Gold recovery is currently at 4.5 grams per ton. Harmony yields 16% per annum.

Hartebeestfontein Gold Mining Co. Ltd. (Harties)
   Shares outstanding: 11,200,000
   Financial year ends June 30.
   Gold profits this year are up 33% for this quality mine. Harties is also a major uranium producer. Grade recovery increased 24% due to an increase in surface sorting rates. Recovery is running at 11.3 grams per ton at a cost of $122 per ounce. In 1972, Harties acquired Zandpan, a marginal producer, yet this acquisition enhanced ore potential; so did a plan to exploit an area in the northeastern part of Vaal Reefs. Harties has a

life expectancy of 20 years. This issue should continue to yield 16% per annum.

Kinross Mines Ltd. (Kinross)
Shares outstanding: 18,000,000
Financial year ends September 30.
The future of this mine depends on results from the No. 2 shaft, and improved overall results, which are now running at 6.2 grams per ton at a cost of $122 per ounce. Other areas of the mine appear promising but grade appears to be low. Kinross should remain sensitive to gold bullion prices, but should perform well if gold remains at present levels. We estimate Kinross to have a 15-year life expectancy.

*Kloof Gold Mining Co. Ltd. (Kloof)
Shares outstanding: 30,240,000
Financial year ends June 30.
Kloof is one of the up-and-coming gold mines in South Africa, with a life expectancy of 25 years. Kloof has suffered from major technical problems over the years, but appears to have resolved these problems and is moving toward production at full capacity. Now, because of high gold prices and improved conditions in the mine, Kloof has a greater degree of flexibility in its operation than it has had for several years. In fact, the mine recently produced at capacity of 180,000 tons per month and improved working profits 22% over the previous quarter. Recovery has risen to 15.1 grams per ton. High spending for capital improvements may limit dividend payouts, but Kloof should be able to pay 14% to 16% annually if gold bullion prices hold at present levels.

Leslie Gold Mines Ltd. (Leslie)
Shares outstanding: 16,000,000
Financial year ends September 30.
Leslie is one of the more interesting leveraged situations, although its life expectancy may be no more than four to five years. Because of higher gold prices, ore reserve estimates have been extended, and although the mine has given a statutory three-month notice of possible foreclosure, state assistance has enabled it to maintain mining operations.
Because of higher gold prices, the marginal areas of the mine can now be exploited. General Mining has approached Leslie

regarding coal mining rights. Leslie is currently showing a gold recovery rate of 4.2 grams per ton and a cost of $168 per ounce. Bracken and Leslie are now working under joint management. If bullion prices remain at present levels, we expect that Leslie can continue to pay a return of 25% to 30% to the investor.

Libanon Gold Mining Co. Ltd. (Libanon)
   Shares outstanding: 7,937,300
   Financial year ends June 30.
Because of high prices for gold, this mine has been able to develop more marginal areas of the property and has now bolstered its reserves. We consider Libanon to be a medium life mine with an expectancy of 13 to 15 years of production. If gold can maintain present price levels, this mining issue should yield 16% per annum.

Loraine Gold Mines Ltd. (Loraine)
   Shares outstanding: 16,366,986
   Financial year ends September 30.
In order for Loraine to sustain its mining operations, it must maintain high production to offset a continuous drop in ore grade recovery, now running at 5 grams per ton at an exorbitant cost of $310.50 per ounce. This mine relies heavily on state aid in order to continue operating. It is uncertain whether Loraine will declare a dividend in the near future. Speculator demand now thrives on the hope of a future dividend payment, and the effect that this may have on share prices.

Marievale Consolidated Mines Ltd. (Marievale or Maries)
   Shares outstanding: 4,500,000
   Financial year ends December 31.
Marievale, now nearing the end of the mine's productive life, is treating mainly surface rock dumps. Underground operation is marginal at best. Therefore, after 1979, operations will consist of milling low-grade ore from surface dumps, clean-up operations, and disposal of assets. At best we can hope for reasonable revenue at breakup value.

*President Brand Gold Mining Co. Ltd. (Brand's)
   Shares outstanding: 14,040,000
   Fiscal year ends September 30.

Uranium has become very important to the earnings of this mine, as President Brand is the focal point of Anglo American's Joint Metallurgical Scheme. Capital expenditures are being geared toward increased production of Brand's uranium plant. The southwestern part of the mine has shown marginal results for gold ore recovery, and therefore grade recovery may decline from current levels of 9.3 grams per ton at a cost of $112.97 per ounce. Capital expenditures will remain high in order to maintain a 15- to 16-year life expectancy. If gold prices remain at present levels, the mine may continue to yield 16% per annum.

President Steyn Gold Mining Co. Ltd. (Steyn's)
   Shares outstanding: 14,566,400
   Fiscal year ends September 30.
   Steyn's is also a member of the Joint Metallurgical Scheme of Anglo American. Though uranium earnings should prove to be important, very encouraging results have developed in the southern area of the mine. Assuming gold prices at close to present levels and an increase in production during the next 2 years, this mine should have a life expectancy of 15 to 16 years and pay 16% per annum over the next few years.

The Randfontein Estates Gold Mining Co. Witwatersrand Ltd. (Randfontein or Rand)
   Shares outstanding: 5,413,553
   Fiscal year ends December 31.
   Randfontein remains one of the higher-quality mines in South Africa and may soon become one of its largest uranium producers as well. Though 1979 recorded several production problems which will affect earnings, the Cooke section of the Randfontein mine promises a bright future. It will be interesting to see if high gold prices will enable Rand to increase its payout beyond the present 11%. Although grade recovery has fallen to 5.5 grams per ton and cost has risen to $163.32 per ounce, Rand's long-term prospects remain bright.

Saint Helena Gold Mines Ltd. (Saints)
   Shares outstanding: 9,625,000
   Financial year ends September 30.
   St. Helena has experienced a sharp drop in grade during the last few years, yet good results are expected from the northern area of the mine. As grade recovery drops from 9.0 grams per

ton, costs will rise from the current level of $98.61 per ounce. St. Helena will remain highly sensitive to gold bullion price fluctuations. If prices remain where they are, this mine can be expected to pay a 16% yield for a few more years.

Southvaal Holdings Ltd. (Southvaal)
   Shares outstanding: 26,000,000
   Financial year ends December 31.
   Southvaal is not a mine but a financial company that receives 55% of the royalties from Vaal Reefs' development of the South Lease area of the Vaal Reefs mine. Southvaal's property has long life expectancy, along with high-grade uranium ore. Grade recovery runs at 10.8 grams per ton at a cost of $112.60 per ounce. Southvaal pays a dividend only once a year; if gold's price continues to be favorable, Southvaal's payout may become competitive with those of other mines.

Stilfontein Gold Mining Co. Ltd. (Stils)
   Shares outstanding: 13,062,920
   Financial year ends December 31.
   Stils is one of the more interesting marginal situations because it is also very heavily involved with uranium production. A large plant has just been completed ahead of schedule and the mine is processing slimes at 80% of capacity. This mine has also been able to develop lower areas of its structure, and has boosted recovery grade to 8.4 grams per ton at a cost of $180.85 per ounce. We expect this mine to continue both gold and uranium production for at least 5 more years; assuming continued high bullion prices, it should continue to pay 14% to 16% in dividends.

Unisel Gold Mines Ltd. (Unisel)
   Shares outstanding: 28,000,000
   Financial year ends September 30.
   This mine has recently begun production, and having its ore treated by the St. Helena facility. As a young mine, it will experience high capital expenditures. Ore grade is expected to be marginal. If gold remains high and capital expenditures are not excessive, this mine should begin paying dividends reasonably soon.

Vaal Reefs Exploration and Mining Co. Ltd. (Vaals)
  Shares outstanding: 19,000,000
  Financial year ends December 31.

Vaals is South Africa's second largest gold producer, responsible for 10% of South Africa's gold output and its largest uranium producer with 25% of the nation's production. Vaals has begun to exploit the Afrikander Lease property for which it will receive royalties. Vaals is a massive operation employing almost 50,000 laborers. Its average recovery grade is 8.2 grams per ton at at cost of $148.28 per ounce. It should continue to pay its investors 16% annually. Recommended for any shareholder's portfolio.

Venterspost Gold Mining Co. Ltd. (Venterspost or Venters)
  Shares outstanding: 5,050,000
  Financial year ends June 30.

Venters is a marginal mine at best and has a short life expectancy. This mine has been on state assistance for the last three years, yet with higher gold prices and projected higher tonnages, could offset the effects of declining grade, now 4.8 grams per ton, and high cost, now $246.11 per ounce. Third-quarter 1979 profits were favorable, and if gold does maintain present levels, an investor may look for more favorable dividend payouts.

Welkom Gold Mining Co. Ltd. (Welkom)
  Shares outstanding: 12,250,000
  Financial year ends September 30.

Welkom has shifted quite a bit of its attention in recent years to uranium and is also involved in Anglo American's Joint Metallurgical Scheme. Its current ore reserves for gold can be termed marginal. It needs a bullion price of $220 an ounce to break even, so existing gold prices provide a margin of comfort. Anglo American has considered involving Welkom in the development of several marginal mines north of Free State Saaiplaas. Recovery is at 5.5 grams per ton at a cost of $188.17 per ounce. At current gold prices, a 16% payout can be maintained.

West Driefontein Gold Mining Co. Ltd. (West Dries)
  Shares Outstanding: 14,082,160
  Financial year ends June 30.

West Dries is truly the giant of gold mines; with a labor force of 50,000 it is South Africa's largest gold mine, with the highest ore grade recovery (20.3 grams per ton) and a low cost ($64.23 per ounce). West Dries enjoyed its most profitable quarter in the July-September period of 1979. West Dries is South Africa's second largest uranium producer, after Vaals. The 16% payout is expected to be maintained, and shares in this mine are recommended for every portfolio.

West Rand Consolidated Mines Ltd. (West Rand)
Shares outstanding: 4,250,000 common; 25,000 preferred
Financial year ends December 31.

West Rand has now become a primary uranium producer through the acquisition of the old Luipaardsvlei from Gold Fields and its continuous milling of uranium ore at the millsite. Gold reserves are marginal at best, with grade recovery dropping sharply to 3.0 grams per ton and at marginal recovery costs. West Rand is an interesting speculation in the leverage category.

Western Areas Gold Mining Co. Ltd. (Western Areas)
Shares outstanding: 40,306,950
Financial year ends December 31.

Western Areas is another marginal gold mine which has become interested in uranium, so much so that Nufcor has inquired about assisting in the construction of a plant and entering into long-term contracts. The mine is also developing new ways to approach underground levels that may enhance gold reserves. At a grade recovery of 5.3 grams per ton and a cost of $198.62 per ounce, this mine can maintain and possibly increase its 14% payout only with bullion prices at late 1979 levels or higher.

*Western Deep Levels Ltd. (Western Deeps or Deep Levels)
Shares outstanding: 25,000,000
Financial year ends December 31.

Western Deep Levels is probably the deepest mine in South Africa, working ores as deep as 3,050 meters (10,010 ft.), and its operating and capital costs are correspondingly high. However, profits have been encouraging. An extension of a uranium plant is expected to be commissioned early in 1980. Grade recovery has improved sharply to 15.2 grams per ton, and costs are conservative at $95.57 per ounce. Western Deeps should maintain a payout rate of 14% to 16%. This long-life mine is an interesting situation.

Western Holdings Ltd. (Western Holdings or Holdings)
   Shares outstanding: 7,496,376
   Financial year ends September 30.
   Western Holdings has recently been able to increase production, although grade recovery has slipped to 9.9 grams per ton with a cost of $95.75 per ounce of gold. This is a situation that bears careful attention. Holdings is a member of the Joint Metallurgical Scheme, and uranium continues to figure importantly in the mine's future. Holdings may join Welkom in the development of some marginal mines north of Free State Saaiplaas. With gold at late 1979 prices, the mine should continue to pay 14%.

Winklehaak Mines Ltd. (Winkies)
   Shares outstanding: 12,000,000
   Financial year ends September 30.
   Winkies has increased production at the cost of lower grade recovery, now at 7.4 grams per ton and a cost of $90.79. However, exploitation of the northern mine area is promising. Winkies has arranged a deal with Union Corp. to acquire the eastern bloc, which could have positive results. Winkies is expected to continue paying 14% while gold maintains its present price.

Witwatersrand Nigel (Wits)
   Shares outstanding: 7,974,721
   Financial year ends June 30.
   Wits is a marginal mine and remains sensitive to bullion price fluctuations. High gold prices prompted an increase in production. With a grade recovery of only 3.9 grams per ton and a cost of $294.95 per ounce, dividends can be maintained only at relatively high bullion prices.

Chapter 9

North American Gold Shares

"All major crises have been caused by previous inflation, which is far from being isolated and which, sooner or later, leads to collapse."

—*Dr. Friedrich A. von Hayek,*
co-winner of 1974 Nobel Prize in Economics

AN INVESTOR WISHING to diversify his positions in precious metals may consider buying shares in North American mining companies. The geological, economic, and political factors influencing these shares are far different from those affecting South African securities. The risk-reward factors are sharply different.

For the non-Communist world, the U.S., Canada, and Mexico collectively are second only to South Africa in the production of gold, accounting for about 20 percent of Free World output. North America, of course, is a rich source of other mineral wealth. The U.S. is the world's leading producer of uranium and copper; Mexico leads the Free World in silver production, with the U.S. a close second. Canada is second only to South Africa as a Free World producer of platinum, and both Canada and the U.S. are major sources of other important industrial minerals.

The Attraction of Stability

Though most North American gold mines are marginal, high-cost producers in comparison with the great mines of South Africa, they gain attractiveness because of the stable political climate in which they operate. Thus, purely political tensions are less likely to skew investor psychology and share prices for North American investments. It is a common observation that political tensions viewed as possibly affecting South African production tend to push the price of gold upward, but this does not translate into higher share prices for South African companies. On the other hand, higher gold prices do tend to improve prices for North American shares.

Along with the lower political risk in North American shares goes a markedly lower dividend yield. Working profits from the mines must account for future labor costs, high taxes, and high costs for capital expenditures. Therefore, the attraction of the

North American issues lies more in their growth prospects than in their immediate yields.

Most of the North American mining companies are either independent operations financed by venture capital or are subsidiaries of major U.S. or Canadian mining companies. The geology of the ores is notably different from those in South African mines, and so are the methods of exploitation. Ore quality is generally lower in North America.

View from the Markets

Investment characteristics are different as well. The North American mining issues are generally listed on major stock exchanges or are traded in over-the-counter markets. Thus, some of the issues may be bought on margin. Most of the Canadian mining issues are listed on the Toronto, Montreal, or Vancouver stock exchanges, and trade over-the-counter in the U.S. Typically, North American issues have far fewer shares outstanding than do the big South African issues.

During the latter half of 1979, the South African shares enjoyed the most favorable market behavior they have experienced in five years. Most of the shares have given strong performances and are well above their lows for the year. In North America, some companies have gained a new lease on life because of high bullion prices that make the mining of marginal properties economically feasible. In other cases, properties passed over earlier because of their low-grade ore are getting fresh consideration for development. Many of these speculative issues carry market prices of less than $1 a share; other mines selling in this range earlier in 1979 have moved up to $10 a share.

There are probably other situations capable of this type of growth, but careful research and investigation are advisable before making a commitment. Promotion men are sometimes paid by mine owners to "talk" a stock to higher levels. Such ventures are highly speculative, and the prospective buyer should exercise the greatest caution before investing.

If gold and silver bullion can maintain prices close to their late 1979 levels, then some of these speculative ventures may actually go into production and turn a profit, and formerly marginal mines can show improved performances. North American precious metals shares are expected to reflect sensitivity to the market prices of the metals themselves, as well as to the prices of other minerals that the mines recover as by-products.

Here are some notable gold and silver mining issues that may benefit from production of other valuable raw materials:

Gold Stocks

Agnico Eagle Mines Ltd.
Shares outstanding: 13,861,827.
Financial year ends December 31.
Exchanges: Toronto, Montreal; U.S. Over-the-Counter
Agnico is a gold and silver mine, where the gold operation works out of the Joutel Township in Quebec and the silver property in the South Lorrain Township in Ontario. The mine is also involved in milling cobalt, which was valued in 1978 at $1,600,000. Agnico and Noranda have entered into a joint development agreement at Agnico's property in Cobalt, Ontario. Noranda will receive 49% of royalties. Earnings for 1979 were running 50% over 1978, because of gold and silver recoveries. In March 1979, Agnico declared its first dividend, a payment of 10 cents a share. This yield should improve as mining results continue to improve. This mine has no long-term debt.

Camflo Mines Ltd.
Shares outstanding: 3,533,307
Financial year ends December 31.
Exchanges: Toronto, Montreal; U.S. Over-the-Counter
Camflo is a gold producer located near the town of Malartic, Quebec; it has a mill capacity of 1,250 tons a day, capable of producing more than 75,000 ounces of gold a year. Camflo has a 25% share of the Kashmere Lake Joint Venture in Manitoba with United Siscoe, a company in which Camflo owns a 22% interest. United Siscoe is also involved in oil and gas exploration and in uranium development. Camflo participates in oil and gas exploration through Signalta, Voyager, Renaissance, and Orbit joint ventures. Camflo also owns 23% of Wilanour Resources, a gold mine producing ore at the rate of 400 tons a day.

Campbell Red Lake Mines Ltd.
   Shares outstanding: 15,998,000
   Financial year ends March 30.
   Exchanges: Toronto and New York Stock Exchange.
   CRK, as it is known, is North America's largest and most
efficient gold producer, with a production of more than 185,000
ounces a year, double the production of Dome Mines, the second-ranking producer. CRK is involved in a joint exploration
program for gold with Dome, Sigma, and Dome Petroleum, and
through partial ownership of Denison Mines participates in
uranium production. The company has no long-term debt.

Dickenson Mines Ltd.
   Shares outstanding: 4,092,774
   Financial year ends December 31.
   Exchange: Toronto; U.S. Over-the-Counter
   Dickenson owns a gold-producing property in the Red Lake
area of Ontario, with a mill capacity of 480 tons a day. The
company's subsidiaries include Abino Gold, Craibbe-Fletcher
Gold, New Cinch Uranium, and Conventures Ltd., and an oil
and gas exploration company in Calgary.

Dome Mines Ltd.
   Shares outstanding: 19,320,012
   Financial year ends December 31.
   Exchanges: Toronto, Montreal, NYSE, and Paris.
   Dome Petroleum purchased 547,183 shares of Dome Mines
this year to increase its interest to 40% of the latter company.
Dome Mines controls 57% of Campbell Red Lake and 63% of
Sigma. Dome owns 26% of Dome Petroleum; it has no outstand-
ing debt.

Giant Yellowknife Mines Ltd.
   Shares outstanding: 4,303,050.
   Financial year ends December 31.
   Exchanges: Toronto and American Stock Exchange.
   Giant Yellowknife has a mill with capacity of 1,000 tons of
ore a day on its property near Yellowknife Bay in the Northwest
Territories; it also controls a number of gold-mining subsidiar-
ies.

Homestake Mining Co.
Shares outstanding: 11,337,934
Financial year ends December 31.
Exchanges: NYSE
Homestake is the leading U.S. gold producer and in 1978 enjoyed a 63% gain in income, largely because of improved gold
prices. Also because of an improved market, Homestake has
upgraded the value of its ore reserves. Homestake is involved
in the production of other industrial minerals, including uranium; in its uranium production it is a co-partner with United
Nuclear.

Painour Porcupine Mines Ltd.
Shares outstanding: 7,000,000
Financial year ends December 31.
Exchange: Toronto; U.S. Over-the-Counter
This mine operates a 3000-ton-a-day milling plant on its principal property and two other mills rated at 750 and 400 tons a
day, all in the Porcupine area of Ontario. Painour also controls
a number of subsidiaries that are gold and copper producers.

Sigma Mines Ltd.
Shares outstanding: 2,000,000
Financial year ends December 31.
Exchanges: Toronto, Montreal; U.S. Over-the-Counter
Sigma operates a gold property in the Val d'Or area in Que-
bec; it participates with Dome Mines in various joint ventures.
The company held 200,000 shares of Dome Mines and 461,700
shares of Denison Mines, and 60,624 shares of Panartic Oils
Ltd. Sigma is responsible for a full 10% of all exploration in
Canada outside of Quebec and Ontario, and accounts for 6% of
the exploration in Quebec.

Some other North American producers:

Rosario
This is one of the largest producers of silver in the world,
owning silver mines in Honduras and in the Dominican Republic, and it owns Fresnillo in Mexico. It is diversified into oil
and gas through its subsidiary, Alamo Petroleum Company, in
Alberta, Canada. Rosario recently acquired 20% of Hecla Min-

ing. With its shares at 37¼, Rosario yields a dividend return of 2%.

Callahan Mining

Callahan operates the Galena Mine in the Coeur d'Alene district of Idaho, the second largest silver mine in the U.S., and for this service received 50% royalties from the mine's operator, Asarco. For the first half of 1979, revenues were up 50% from the previous year. Callahan owns Pinnacle Exploration, a uranium mining project in Colorado.

Chapter 10

Silver, Platinum, and Palladium

"The budget should be balanced, the Treasury should be refilled, public debt should be reduced, the arrogance of officialdom should be tempered and controlled, and the assistance to foreign lands should be curtailed lest Rome become bankrupt. The mobs should be forced to work and not depend on government for substance."

—*Cicero,*
addressing the Roman Senate

IF YOU PLAY the game of word association and you mention coffee, the average person will say tea. Mention gold and silver comes to mind.

This isn't surprising for silver, like gold, has a colorful history, has performed monetary functions, and has important industrial uses. However, unlike gold it has been successfully downgraded as a monetary metal.

To put it in perspective, it might be said that gold is the star player in the pageant of metals; silver is one of the supporting cast. As some professionals prefer to look at it, silver holds an intermediate position between gold—the prime monetary metal—and copper—the prime industrial metal.

Although silver is unlikely ever to rival gold's mystique, it can be a dazzling commodity at times. Early in 1974, its price rose to a new high level of $6.40 an ounce, having doubled in two months' time. This price induced holders of old coins to bring their hoards out of hiding and into the market place, and this helped to restrain the price. In fact, silver did not return to such a lofty level until 1979.

Speculative pressures, inflation fears, and the continuing flight of investors from paper money and securities into tangible goods all helped to account for silver's 1979 price surge. One of the extraordinary factors was the widespread rumor that a Texas millionaire had a huge speculative position in silver, reportedly amounting to nearly $400 million. All these elements, plus the tightening noose on the Free World's energy supply by the OPEC countries, helped push silver to new stratospheric levels.

One peculiarity of the world silver market is that for many years consumption of the metal in the non-communist world has far exceeded mine production. The balance has appeared from salvage, from the melting of old coins, from government stocks, and from the enormous hoard that citizens of India have accumulated over the centuries. Withdrawals from Indian stocks accounted for nearly 9 percent of all silver consumed in the non-communist world in 1978, but in February 1979 the Indian government embargoed the export of silver in an apparent effort to push world prices even higher. If that was the intent, it was successful, and by September and October 1979, silver touched a new price peak of $18.50 an ounce, more than three times its price at the beginning of the year.

Silver's sensitivity to news events and to emotions, rather than to statistics, is well known. Treasury officials have commented on the fact that the price of silver has managed to climb at times when the government was a heavy seller of the metal, then paradoxically the price collapsed after the government halted its sales.

Gyrations in price, often unforeseen and unpredictable, must be regarded as one of the characteristics of the silver market. Nevertheless, it is often helpful to seek to balance the forces affecting the price of silver in order to assess its future price possibilities.

The influences tending to support continued relatively high prices for silver may be summarized as follows:

1. The deterioration of the international financial and monetary picture suggests a continued stampede into all valuable commodities, of which silver is a prime example.

2. Strength in world gold prices usually has a constructive impact on silver, its sister metal.

3. Statistics show a consistent imbalance between production and use of silver. In 1978, for example, new silver production satisfied only 63 percent of the world's demand for industrial use and coinage, reducing available stocks from an estimated 758.4 million ounces to 743.4 million ounces at the end of the year.

4. The pattern of silver consumption shows cyclical trends. In the early 1970s, consumption of silver for commemorative medals and medallions took a great leap, but has since declined as the public's fascination with these objects has cooled. While the medallions seemed to satisfy the collecting instinct of millions and to offer an interesting pastime, they are a poor method of hoarding or investing in silver, since the objects are invariably priced far above the value of their silver content.

5. The conventional industrial uses of silver—notably photography and the electrical and electronics field—account for more than 60 percent of all U.S. silver consumption. The manufacture of silverware and jewelry and the use of silver as a

chemical catalyst account for most of the other consumption.

Some factors that will tend to limit further price increases in silver are these:

1. The U.S. government still has substantial quantities of the metal in its stockpile and it could release much of this for sale.

2. During recessionary periods, silver prices tend to weaken because of reduced industrial demand. In each of the last two recessions (1970–71 and 1974–75), silver consumption in the U.S. showed notable dips from pre-recession peaks.

3. More than 65 percent of newly produced silver comes as a by-product of the mining of copper, zinc, lead, and other base metals. In effect, this means that the supply and demand for these base metals influence silver production more than the supply and demand for silver itself. The great bulk of any new silver production, therefore, would have to come from increased base metal operations. Demand for base metals continues to grow, and this increases the supply of new silver coming to the market.

A Volatile Metal

It is reasonable to expect that wide price swings, frequently dictated by emotional and psychological factors, will continue in the silver market. Consider that in 1964 a teaspoon in sterling contained about one ounce of silver worth $1.29. In 1974 the value of the silver in that teaspoon touched a peak market value of $6.70, a record that was to last until 1979, when a new surge pushed silver to the $18 level.

Silver Prices
(New York)

	High	Low	Average
1979*	$18.00	$5.96	(not available)
1978	6.30	4.83	$5.40
1977	4.96	4.30	4.62
1976	5.10	3.82	4.35
1975	5.23	3.91	4.42
1974	6.70	3.27	4.71
1973	3.28	1.96	2.56
1972	2.05	1.39	1.68
1971	1.75	1.29	1.55
1970	1.93	1.57	1.77

Source: Handy & Harman   *Through October 1979

World Silver Consumption
(excluding communist-dominated areas)
(millions of ounces)

	1978	1977	1976	1975	1974
Industrial uses:					
United States	159.5	153.6	170.5	157.7	177.0
Canada	9.0	8.8	9.5	10.6	9.6
Mexico	5.8	5.5	6.5	5.6	5.0
United Kingdom	29.0	32.0	28.0	28.0	25.0
France	22.2	20.6	19.0	21.2	15.5
West Germany	26.4	33.8	50.8	38.9	59.9
Italy	26.0	27.0	28.2	28.9	38.6
Japan	64.3	62.7	60.7	46.4	46.5
India	20.0	17.6	18.0	13.0	15.0
Other countries	25.8	25.5	26.9	26.5	16.9
Total industrial uses	388.0	387.1	418.2	376.8	409.0
Coinage:					
United States	.1	.4	1.3	2.7	1.0
Canada	.3	.3	8.4	10.4	8.9
Austria	9.5	7.0	6.9	13.4	5.6
France	11.1	6.9	6.7	5.2	.1
West Germany	3.6	2.4	2.9	4.3	8.8
Other countries	10.4	6.0	3.5	2.8	3.5
Total coinage	35.0	23.0	29.7	38.8	27.9
Total Consumption	423.0	410.1	447.9	415.6	436.9

Source: Handy & Harman

The volatility of silver has caused some industries—notably photography—to devote considerable effort to finding a cheap silver substitute. Whether this eventually comes about is a moot question; in the foreseeable future, it can be argued that silver accounts for only a small portion of the material costs of photography-oriented companies and therefore, for these firms, price swings in the metal are not as significant as they might seem to be.

In general, it is our conclusion that while silver is scarcely on a par with gold as a haven against currency inflation and "Lazyfare" economics, and involves an appreciable degree of price risk, the metal cannot and will not be ignored.

During periods of market weakness, opportunities will arise to take silver positions, but those unfamiliar with trading techniques should be sure to avail themselves of competent advice before dabbling in this volatile market.

For the speculative-minded, the silver futures markets in New York, Chicago, and London offer the biggest potential rewards, with commensurate risks. A typical transaction on the Chicago Board of Trade, for example, could generate a 62 percent profit on a 5 percent rise in silver prices, but of course, this type of leverage also works in reverse.

Direct purchases of silver also may be made through banks or brokers. The silver is usually sold in bricks with officially listed brands or markings. A 1,000-ounce brick is about the size of a loaf of bread and weighs about eighty-three pounds; smaller bricks of 100, 10, and even one ounce also are available. In view of storage problems and insurance costs, we would advise against taking physical possession of large quantities of silver.

Perennial Problems

A few final words about silver.

There are some perennial problems faced by the silver speculator that should be recognized.

One is the uncertain reliability of much of the data that is available concerning the metal. Although Handy & Harman, the world's largest silver dealer, and the Bureau of Mines provide a great volume of useful statistics, fundamental data on silver for much of the world is of dubious quality. This can lead to erroneous and conflicting conclusions, depending upon which source of information you use. Also some bullion dealers have a bias in favor of their prime customers (industrial), who naturally favor lower prices. So treat their comments with suspicion.

Second, we would caution against any rule-of-thumb approaches to analyzing the silver market. For instance the so-called silver-gold ratio has practically no value as a forecasting tool despite assertions to the contrary. The ratio of about 32 to 1 in favor of gold that existed in 1978, for example, might be considered to be relatively high in comparison with the 20- or 30-to-1 ratios that have existed for a large part of the past two decades. But we would apply no particular significance to this ratio as it is too susceptible to statistical aberration. It is, in any case, not a timing mechanism—and thus useless.

Finally we would caution against placing silver in the same class as gold as a hedge against political and fiscal irresponsibility. Silver has great charisma, no question about that, but, unfortunately, it is also a highly volatile commodity with a limited role to play as a monetary metal.

The Place of Platinum

Many people interested in gold and silver also find platinum, and to a lesser extent, palladium, captivating. A brief mention of these metals is in order.

Platinum, a whitish, steel-gray element, has a high melting point, exceptional resistance to corrosion, and—perhaps most important in terms of today's market—exceptional catalytic properties.

Platinum began to find favor in the early 1900s, when it was employed as a lining for chemical vessels and in various other industrial uses. In the 1920s, International Nickel Co. began to produce platinum as a by-product of nickel, and this opened new vistas for the metal.

A major breakthrough occurred in the 1930s when a platinum-rhodium catalyst was utilized in producing nitric acid. Another breakthrough came with the development of platinum nozzles containing microscopic holes for use in manufacturing synthetic fibers.

Later, platinum assumed a significant role in the refining and automobile industries. Oil industry researchers found that a platinum catalyst filled a vital role in the manufacture of high-octane gasoline. In recent years the mandatory use of emission-control devices in automobiles sold in the U.S. opened a major new market for the metal, and by 1978 accounted for about half of all the platinum consumed in the U.S.

Worldwide, petroleum and automobile manufacturing together account for close to one-third of all platinum consumption. Impala Platinum, the world's second-largest producer of the metal, has stated that "demand by the automobile industry for platinum (and palladium) for catalytic converters will, for some years, provide a relatively stabilizing element in the market for these metals which in the past has been notable for wide fluctuations."

In Japan, where the annual consumption of platinum is comparable to that of the U.S. (around 1.1 million ounces in recent years), the jewelry industry is the major consumer, absorbing more than two-thirds of the platinum used. There are some indications that the extraordinarily high prices reached by platinum in 1979 may have reduced consumption by the Japanese jewelry industry.

It has been estimated that by 1980, world demand for platinum will approach 3 million ounces annually, up some 20 percent from 1976. By far, the biggest source of supply is South Africa, which controls about 75 percent of the world's known mining reserves and accounts for about half the world's production. Most of the remaining supply comes from the Soviet Union and in recent years was subject to unpredictable marketing practices. In 1978, for reasons that were never fully explained, the Soviet Union cut back its sales to the West by some 400,000 ounces. Some observers thought the Soviet Union might have withheld platinum in order to create an issue of special coins commemorating the 1980 Olympics in Moscow. The Soviet Union's own expanding consumption of platinum for its internal chemical and fertilizer industries also absorbed large amounts of the metal.

The shortage had a predictably bullish effect on the price of platinum. From a level of $180 an ounce at the beginning of 1978, the price soared to $300 at year's end and continued on the same trend into 1979, pushing the price up to a record intra-day high of $700 an ounce, retreating later in the year from that height.

Because platinum is often a by-product of other metal production (copper in the Soviet Union, nickel in Canada), production from those sources does not respond quickly or automatically to increased demand for platinum, and short-term imbalances in the market such as occurred in 1978 can produce sharp price fluctuations. Still, South African mines, where platinum is a prime product, can assure a reasonably steady supply of the metal to Western users. Increasing demand for chemical, electronic, and other manufacturing applications, plus the bullish market factors affecting all precious metals, suggest that platinum will enjoy a strong market and firm prices for the next several years.

The Palladium Picture

Palladium—like platinum, rhodium, iridium, ruthenium, and osmium—is a member of the so-called platinum group of metals. Palladium is silver-white, malleable, and ductile and does not tarnish in air. Palladium is harder than platinum, for which it sometimes serves as a substitute.

Some industries substitute palladium for gold, depending upon the relative prices of the two metals. In fact, palladium tends to be rather closely correlated in price with gold, whereas the price of platinum appears to move in closer relationship with silver.

The principal markets for palladium are in the electrical, chemical, dental and medical, jewelry, and decorative industries. It is an interesting precious metal, but from an investment or speculative point of view it commands less attention than gold, silver, or platinum.

Chapter 11

Conclusions, Recommendations, Predictions

"Between trusting in the natural stability of gold and the natural stability of the honesty and intelligence of the members of government, I advise you to vote for gold."
—*George Bernard Shaw*

ECONOMISTS HAVE DISCOVERED that consumers as a group possess an uncanny sense of how the economy will move in the months ahead. The business-oriented Conference Board and the University of Michigan's Survey Research Center have used this fact as a forecasting tool, and they regularly survey consumer attitudes and buying plans and construct a "confidence index" to help estimate economic trends. By late 1974, consumer confidence in the U.S. had sunk to the lowest level in the survey's 28-year experience. On a scale using February 1966 as a base of 100, consumer confidence sank to 64.5. Largely on the basis of these findings, the Center forecast a long, deep recession.

The forecast turned out to be quite accurate. As it happened, some unforeseen events served to deepen the recession. One, of course, was the quadrupling of oil prices after the 1973–74 OPEC embargo. Another was the action of the Federal Reserve. In 1974, as the economy appeared ready to start its recovery, the Fed applied new clamps on the money supply in an effort to restrain inflation. The action served to tame the price increases, but it put such a squeeze on the money supply that for several months the money aggregates shrank rather than expanding. This sequence of planned and random events helped to plunge the U.S. into its worst recession since the 1930s.

In late 1979, many economic signs bore an eerie parallel to those of 1974. In September 1979, the University of Michigan Center's consumer confidence index was down to 66.7. Oil prices were on the rise, and inflation rates were higher even than 1974's peak levels. Economists are almost unanimous in expecting a recession in 1980. The University of Michigan Center thinks it will be "moderate and protracted." Jeffrey Green of IMTRAC, a Kansas City–based firm monitoring economic trends, foresees a "double dip recession," in which an early recovery may be set back in mid-1980 by heavy Fed restraint on the money supply. The depth and extent of the expected recession may depend on unforeseen random factors, such as

OPEC's price actions on oil, and the intensity of the Fed's monetary restrictions. The Fed's new chairman, Paul Volcker, has used the elements of surprise and unpredictability to add force to his actions, and the direction and extent of the Fed's money-controlling measures will influence the depth and intensity of the recession.

Despite their overextended positions, the world's central banks are scarcely powerless. They can and will move to meet crisis situations. If they open up the money spigot and reinflate, they could keep things going for quite a while, though this would merely be buying time at the cost of currency debasement. It is our opinion that this will happen.

There is a saying in Wall Street that "the Fed writes the market letter," and it is undeniably true. The Federal Reserve System, after all, determines how much General Motors or A.T.&T. have to pay to float their bonds, as well as the interest rate individuals must accept on their home mortgages. With that kind of power, the Fed can either slow the economy further or stimulate it.

Which course will it take? If the past is any guide, there is no question that inflation—not deflation—is the most politically acceptable mechanism to deal with the painful process of economic adjustment. Furthermore, new social legislation requires reflation and thus more demand is built into law.

Who can doubt that politicians will follow the exhortations of the Keynesian economists and opt for more inflation? Political and social realities limit the extent of the Federal Reserve's anti-inflationary interest rate program. Their effects will result eventually in more rather than less inflationary pressure. In the environment that we have seen in the late 1970s, Federal Reserve actions that increased the cost of money without limiting its supply served to worsen, not control, inflation. In the mortgage market, only the usury laws choke off supplies of credit; the same holds true for consumer credit.

In this connection we find these observations of the 1974 Nobel prize-winning economist Friedrich von Hayek extraordinarily illuminating:

> The responsibility for current worldwide inflation, I am sorry to say, rests wholly and squarely with the economists, or at least with that great majority of my fellow economists who have embraced the teachings of Lord Keynes. . . .

It was on his advice and even urging of his pupils that governments everywhere have financed increasing parts of their expenditure by creating money on a scale which every reputable economist before Keynes would have predicted would cause precisely the sort of inflation we have got. They did this in the erroneous belief that this was both a necessary and lastingly effective method of securing full employment.

The seductive doctrine that a government deficit, as long as unemployment existed, was not only innocuous but even meritorious was of course most welcome to politicians. The advocates of this policy have long maintained that an increase of total expenditure which still led to an increase of employment could not be regarded as inflation at all.[1]

We find this passage even more meaningful now than when it was written in 1974.

One of the most striking failures of the Western world in recent times has been its inability to produce outstanding leaders in the Churchillian mold. Change does not necessarily beget improvement, but somewhere in the current crop of political characters there could be some talented people. Let us continue to hope.

In overall investment strategy we take leave of some contemporaries, to whom gold is the ultimate answer to all problems. We have made gold a cornerstone of investment policy, not a religion.

In our view gold is a monetary commodity with universal attraction from an intrinsic as well as a psychological standpoint. As Janos Fekete, Vice-Chairman of the National Bank of Hungary, has remarked, there are about 300 economists in the world who are against gold, but about 3 billion inhabitants of the world who believe in gold.

We concur. We also are convinced that the failure to return to a system in which there is some provision for gold convertibility, plus control over the creation of paper currency, dooms the world to continuing inflation. And inflation, in the words of Pulitzer prize-winner William Caldwell, "has put poverty within reach of all of us."

Possible Remedies

There are some specific measures to ameliorate our economic ills and set the stage for a return to a sound dollar, which would, in turn, help other currencies:

1. Following an increase in the official price of gold to a figure moderately above the free market price, there should be partial convertibility of gold into dollars.

2. There should be a legal restrike of a gold coin in the United States.

3. Requirements for gold cover and gold convertibility should be reinstated in order to limit increases in the money supply and thereby remove the greatest cause of currency inflation.

4. We should consider establishing a 5 percent band in which the currencies could fluctuate 2½ percent up and 2½ percent down.

5. We should also face the task of reversing the influences that have led to runaway inflation by reducing government spending and balancing the budget.

6. The rate of increase in the money supply should be severely restricted in a consistent application of gradual reduction.

7. Despite the urgings of those who press the panic button when unemployment creeps past 5 percent, we should strenuously avoid taking any measures that will tend to heat up the economy.

We would also recommend that steps be taken toward adopting some form of indexation—the system that links prices, wages, and interest rates to a measurement of the overall price level. It is, in simple terms, an adjustment for inflation. Since politicians simply will not "bite the bullet" in combating inflation, the only solution is to provide some method that adjusts both prices and wages to an overall inflation measurement.

Indexation has worked well in Brazil where capital previously was virtually unobtainable. Belgium has experimented with it and France's Giscard d'Estaing has suggested that it could be used to guarantee the revenues of oil producers.

Indexation actually is already a fixture in many areas of the U.S. economy (e.g., many wage contracts are tied to the cost of living), and we are convinced that it is here to stay whether we like it or not. We don't, but that's incidental to the realities of the situation.

Gold's Potential

Inasmuch as we emphasize gold in our investment strategy, we will attempt to delineate our views on future market possibilities for the metal.

There have been many widely varying predictions as to future price levels for gold—anywhere from $150 to $1,000 per ounce has been forecast, depending upon the time frame for the projection.

Of course, gold is not just a commodity but a universal yardstick of value. In the United States the money supply (demand deposits, time deposits, and currency in circulation) is around $940 million. This dwarfs by a ratio of 29 to one the U.S. gold supply at the official rate of $42.22 an ounce, and is even 3.2 times the value of the gold at a market valuation of $380 an ounce.

Clearly, we may discard the official U.S. Treasury price of $42.22 per ounce as an anachronism. We agree with Giscard d'Estaing, who has initiated the abolition of the "absurd fiction" of the official price for gold and has sponsored an agreement by the International Monetary Fund to allow central banks to buy, sell, and count gold reserves "near the realistic market price."

Gold Price Possibilities

A logical base for future projections is the $120-per-ounce price used in the Italian-German loan agreement of 1974, which might be considered a new floor price for gold.

From our studies we extrapolated a short-term (through 1975) trading range of $150 to $228 per ounce, and a longer-term (through mid-1977) price band of $120 to $309 per ounce. Further, we see a maximum gold price of $900—through 1982. We deem this conservative and would rather err in falling short of the top price than overestimating, which is less useful to investors. Also note that this range has a bottom as well as a top, and that means both are possible alternatives.

The oil-enriched Arab nations traditionally have been traders rather than holders of gold, but this policy appears to be changing. Some day they may demand gold for their oil instead of dollars, or convert part of their reserves to gold.

Ultimately, there is no true potential ceiling for gold. It will go as high as paper money goes low. Or, to put it another way, paper money's value is the value of a politician's promise; gold's value is protected by the inability of politicians to manufacture it.

We feel that every portfolio should have a stake in gold as the ultimate hedge against adversity. We anticipate substantial long-term price appreciation in gold; but even if this forecast does not materialize, the following could be the considerations of an intelligent investor. Assume that the gold-oriented portion of an investment portfolio is 25 percent and the remaining

Suggested Ratios for Gold-Oriented Portfolios

	$10,000 Portfolio	$100,000 Portfolio	$500,000 Portfolio	$1 Million Portfolio
Demand Deposits	15%	5%	5%	5%
Eurocurrency Time Dep.	35%	20%	25%	30%
Gold Equities*	30%	40%	40%	35%
Gold Coins & Bullion	10%	15%	15%	10%
U.S. Treasury Bills	10%	10%	5%	5%
Gold Forward Contracts	0%	10%	10%	15%

*As a general rule, we favor approximately 75% of this portfolio component in South African golds and 25% in North American golds.

$10,000 Portfolio

Demand Deposit:
Swiss franc current account
(checking-type account) $1,500

Eurocurrency Time Deposit:
Six-month Swiss franc certificate of deposit   3,500

Gold Equities:
Evenly distributed between:
West Driefontein Gold Mining Ltd.
St. Helena Gold Mines Limited   3,000
Homestake Mining Company

Gold Coins & Bullion:
Austrian 100-Corona   1,000

Money Market Fund:
Cash deposit   1,000

75 percent is allocated to conventional income-producing media. If our views of the future turn out to be correct, the gold portion would appreciate to an incalculable value; if disaster doesn't strike, then the remaining 75 percent of the portfolio should appreciate more than sufficiently to offset any lack of performance in the gold segment.

Portfolio Ratios

The allocations in the accompanying table are suggested for portfolios of $10,000, $100,000, $500,000, and $1 million and

$100,000 Portfolio

Demand Deposit:
Swiss franc current account
    (checking-type account) $5,000
Eurocurrency Time Deposits:
3-month Swiss franc int'l cert. of deposit   10,000
3-month Dutch guilder int'l cert. of deposit   5,000
3-month Deutsche mark int'l cert. of deposit   5,000
Gold Equities (equal dollar amounts):
Homestake Mining Company   10,000
Campbell Red Lake Mines
Agnico-Eagle Mines Limited

Randfontein Estates Gold Mining Limited
West Driefontein Gold Mining Limited   30,000
Free States Geduld Mines Limited
St. Helena Gold Mines Limited
Gold Coin & Bullion:
South African Krugerrand coin   5,000
Austrian 100-Corona coin

Gold bullion stored in Switzerland   10,000
U.S. Treasury Bills:
90-day bills (dollar investment)   10,000
Gold Forward Contracts:
Trading position covering potential commitment on
    $100,000 forward contract
    (Comex Exchange)   10,000

over. The actual percentages, of course, can be tailored to the needs of individual investors in each classification. For instance, those investors who require more income than the recommended portfolio divisions would generate can allocate larger commitments in high-yielding South African Kaffirs.

The size of the individual portfolio has a direct bearing on the manner in which the funds are allocated. For instance a lower-bracket investor should concentrate on coins and (to a lesser extent) bullion while staying out of the futures market entirely.

Generally speaking, we do not recommend gold futures for anyone with a net worth of less than $100,000 and even then

$500,000 Portfolio

Demand Deposit:
Swiss franc current account
    (checking-type account) $25,000

Eurocurrency Time Deposits:
3-month U.S. dollar int'l cert. of deposit   25,000
3-month Swiss franc int'l cert. of deposit   50,000
3-month Deutsche mark int'l cert. of deposit   25,000

Gold Equities:
Homestake Mining Company
Campbell Red Lake Mines Limited
Dome Mines Limited or Sigma or Camflo   50,000
Agnico-Eagle Mines Limited

Randfontein Estates Gold Mining Limited
West Driefontein Gold Mining Limited
East Driefontein Gold Mining Limited   165,000
Free States Geduld Mines Limited
St. Helena Gold Mines Limited

Grootvlei Mining Limited
Loraine Gold Mines Limited   10,000

Gold Coins & Bullion:
South African Krugerrand coin   25,000
Austrian 100-Corona coin   25,000
Gold bullion stored in Switzerland   25,000

U.S. Treasury Bills:
90-day bills (dollar investment)   25,000

Gold Forward Contracts:
Trading position covering potential commitment on
    $500,000 forward contract
    (Comex Exchange)   50,000

this high-risk area should account for a relatively minor share of the total portfolio.

A few final words of caution: Implementation of these portfolio ratios should be in accord with the principles outlined in the individual chapters on coins, bullion, gold futures, etc. Numismatics were covered in Chapter 7. And it goes without saying that anyone with a sizable portfolio should seek out personalized professional guidance to achieve his overall investment objectives.

$1,000,000 Portfolio

Demand Deposit:
Swiss franc current account
   (checking-type account) . . . $50,000

Eurocurrency Time Deposits:
3-month U.S. dollar int'l cert. of deposit . . . 75,000
3-month Swiss franc int'l cert. of deposit . . . 150,000
3-month Deutsche mark int'l cert. of deposit . . . 75,000

Gold Equities:
Homestake Mining Company
Campbell Red Lake Mines Limited
Dome Mines Limited . . . 100,000
Agnico-Eagle Mines Limited
Sigma Mines

Randfontein Estates Gold Mining Limited
West Driefontein Gold Mining Limited
East Driefontein Gold Mining Limited . . . 150,000
Free States Geduld Mines Limited
St. Helena Gold Mines Limited

Witwatersrand Nigel Gold Mining Limited
Loraine Gold Mines Limited
Blyvooruitzicht Gold Mining Limited . . . 50,000
Harmony Gold Mining Limited

Gold Coin & Bullion:
South African Krugerrand coin . . . 25,000
Austrian 100-Corona coin . . . 25,000
Gold bullion stored in Switzerland . . . 50,000

U.S. Treasury Bills:
90-day bills (dollar investment) . . . 100,000

Forward Gold Contracts:
Trading position covering potential commitment on
$1,500,000 forward contracts
   (Comex Exchange) . . . 150,000

Chapter 12

Answers to Twenty Frequently Asked Questions About Gold

When asked about the possibility of a change in the price of gold back in 1958, Prime Minister Harold Macmillan of Great Britain responded:

"That is one of those questions it is even indecent to ask and still more improper to answer."

1. Why have Americans been barred from owning gold when many other countries were permitting their citizens to own the metal?

The ban was triggered by the depression of the 1930s when President Franklin D. Roosevelt initiated a series of measures aimed at restoring confidence and prosperity. Roosevelt decided that we must take "control of the gold value of our dollar" and issued an executive order prohibiting private and bank ownership of gold coins, bullion, and gold certificates. The Gold Reserve Act of 1934 made it official. The prohibition against gold ownership persisted thereafter because U.S. Treasury officials took the position that gold should be "demonetized" or, in simple language, relegated to a minor role in our monetary system. President Kennedy tightened the ban in 1961 by ending the right of U.S. citizens to own gold bullion overseas. President Nixon demonetized gold, ending its role as a monetary control, by removing the gold cover clause.

2. Who are the biggest producers of gold?

South Africa, the Soviet Union, Canada, and the United States in that order. South Africa is far in front with more than 56 percent of estimated 1978 production. The second-ranking producer, Russia, is far behind with 24 percent of estimated output for 1978. Canada's share of production is between 4 percent and 5 percent, while the United States is a relatively minor factor with less than 3 percent.

3. Who are the biggest owners of gold?

The U.S. has a commanding lead, owning more than one-fourth of all the world's known gold, a store of value worth $11.3 billion at the official price of $42.22 an ounce, or just over $100 billion at 1979 market prices. In the non-communist world, West Germany is the second largest owner of gold ($36 billion at 1979 prices), followed by Switzerland ($31.6 billion), France ($31 billion), Italy ($25.2 billion), and the Netherlands ($16.6 billion).

4. How much gold is there in Fort Knox?

About 147 million ounces of the gold owned by the United States are stored in Fort Knox, Kentucky. This is about 55 percent of the 268 million ounces of gold that the U.S. owns. Gold that is not stored in Fort Knox rests in vaults in New York, San Francisco, Denver, and Philadelphia.

5. Do other countries permit ownership and trading of gold?

Yes. Among the many countries permitting their citizens to own gold are West Germany, Japan, Canada, France, Italy, the Netherlands, and Switzerland. The full list is quite long.

6. What are gold's principal uses?

The gold supply in the non-communist countries is absorbed into four principal channels: investment, coinage, and hoarding, accounting for about 29 percent; jewelry, which especially in underdeveloped countries is another form of hoarding, about 58 percent; and industrial uses including dentistry, about 13 percent.

7. How can I protect myself against counterfeit gold?

In several ways. If you take physical possession of gold bullion, insist that it has the assay mark of one of several well-known approved assaying firms. Among them: Engelhard Industries Division of Engelhard Minerals & Chemicals Corp., 430 Mountain Ave., Murray Hill, N.J. 07974; Mathey-Bishop, Inc., Malverne, Pa. 19355; Ledoux & Co., 359 Alfred Ave., Teaneck, N.J. 07666; International Testing Laboratories, Inc., 578 Market St., Newark, N.J. 07105.

If you do not take physical possession, insist on a document attesting to your ownership of the metal and its authenticity. For safeguards in purchasing gold coins see Chapter 7.

8. *Why is there so much hoarding of gold?*

The demand for gold and other precious metals accelerates under conditions of political, economic, and monetary turmoil. In recent times, distrust of paper currencies has increased as a result of high inflation throughout the world, including the U.S. The fear behind these trends was exacerbated by continuing price increases in oil and constant threats against the security of supplies. If these threats were realized, the damage to the economies of the industrialized nations would be incalculable. All of this, plus the failure of the major trading nations of the world to agree on a new world monetary system that would reduce swings in currency values and eliminate the currency devaluations that have marked the postwar period, has intensified the demand for the one standard that seems to retain its value—gold. Gold is "stored sweat" and that is what men want —to be able to put away their earnings to spend at a later date, knowing it will buy as much as when stored. Without that security, bank savings accounts and insurance become a mockery.

9. *What do the leading producers of gold do with their output of the metal?*

South Africa's output is largely shipped to the London and Zurich markets where it is sold at the daily "fixings." However it is anticipated that an increasing proportion of South African gold will go into production of the Krugerrand, a one-ounce gold coin that now absorbs nearly 22 percent of new gold production. According to reports that have not been denied, South Africa has also used its supply of gold to make direct purchases of oil from Middle East producing countries.

10. *What is the difference today between the "free" market price of gold and the "official" U.S. Treasury price?*

The official price of gold, $42.22 per ounce, was set by President Nixon in February 1973 when he devalued the dollar for the second time. It is the price at which the Treasury theoretically stood ready to buy and sell gold, but it must be considered an artificial price because no transactions ever took place at this level.

The "free" market price is the price at which actual transactions have been taking place in the world market. The free market price is set in the London gold market or in Zurich. The London market was originated in 1919 at the offices of N. M. Rothschild & Sons, where market price "fixings" have been held ever since with few interruptions. There are currently five members or dealers in this market, each of whom represents the needs of producers, industry, the arts, speculators, and hoarders. At two meetings each day, which take place at 10:30 A.M. and 3:00 P.M. London time (5:30 A.M. and 10 A.M. New York time), the dealers arrive at a price for gold based on supply and demand.

11. *What significant changes have occurred in the use of gold in financial dealings in recent years?*

In 1971 the United States suspended the convertibility of gold for dollars held by monetary authorities of foreign countries. In December of the same year the United States raised the official price of gold from $35 an ounce (which had prevailed since 1934) to $38 an ounce, thereby devaluating the dollar. In February 1973, the United States further devalued the dollar by setting the official price of gold at $42.22 an ounce. Now, among the major currencies, only the Swiss franc has an official gold backing, in the amount of .21759 grams of fine gold per franc. While not officially backed by gold, the seven currencies of the European Monetary System (Deutsche mark, French franc, Italian lira, Belgian franc, Dutch guilder, Irish pound) are supported by an intervention fund that includes 84.5 million ounces of gold pledged by the member nations.

12. *Where can I buy gold?*

You are able to purchase gold through such outlets as broker-age firms, banks, department stores, and jewelers. In addition, a number of U.S. commodity exchanges are prepared to trade in gold futures, that is, gold for future delivery.

13. *Should I "shop around" if I buy gold?*

Absolutely. You should follow the same general rules that apply to almost any commodity or product. Compare prices asked by sellers, and be sure to ask for an itemization of charges for storage, insurance, assaying, etc. This is especially impor-tant if you are buying gold in small quantities; in such transac-tions the commission will be relatively high and there will be several middlemen taking a profit out of the final price you pay. Be sure to inquire about the procedures that will be required for you to sell the gold back to the original seller.

14. *Should I buy gold bullion, gold coins, gold shares, or trade gold futures?*

It depends upon your needs, interests, and financial capabili-ties. If you are a small investor, you might consider gold coins and/or gold mining shares; if you have sizable capital to invest and can assume a fair degree of risk, then gold bullion and/or gold futures might serve as trading vehicles. In each instance it should be recognized that substantial risks are involved in buying and selling bullion, and especially in the gold futures market. (These gold-oriented investments are covered in indi-vidual chapters of this book.)

15. *Does gold have any drawbacks as an investment?*

The most obvious one, perhaps, is that it produces no income for its owner, who, therefore, is dependent on a rise in price to show a profit. Gold is a highly volatile commodity that will rise or fall in line with changing conditions in the world of interna-tional business and finance.

16. *Will gold rise in price?*

It has risen in the free market from $35 in 1971, to $90 an ounce in September 1973, to $197.50 in December 1974, and in 1979 traded at more than $400 an ounce. During this time the securities markets of the world were generally in a down trend. Estimates of future price trends vary widely. Presently gold appears overpriced at 480–520 and undervalued at 320.

17. *Is the gold market regulated or unregulated?*

Largely unregulated. However, this is not true in the U.S. Congress set up a Commodity Futures Trading Commission, which is to the commodities field what the Securities & Exchange Commission is to the securities business. The five-member CFTC has under its domain such commonly traded commodities as sugar, cocoa, and coffee—as well as silver and gold. Commodity trading advisers, incidentally, also come under the law. The Securities & Exchange Commission so far has indicated that it does not regard gold sales as being subject to the securities laws.

18. *When is the best time to buy gold?*

That is strictly a matter of judgment. There is an old and fairly reliable investment maxim to the effect that it pays to buy on weakness and sell on strength. This seems to be a good rule to apply for anyone who is considering an investment or speculative commitment in gold. If you let your emotions rule you, then you will want to do the opposite. Try to resist the urge.

19. *Where should I keep my gold?*

It depends upon the amount of gold you have purchased and your personal desires. Coins, small bars, and wafers may be kept in a safe deposit box. And a few at home. But it would be unwise to take delivery of a standard 400-ounce gold bar or ingot weighing 33⅓ pounds unless you have exceptional safekeeping facilities. It would be much more convenient for you to instruct the agent who arranged for the purchase to have the gold stored in a commercial bank or other depository. Citibank (N.Y.), for example, is a full-service depository, licensed to issue receipts on the Commodity Exchange of New York, the New York Mercantile Exchange, and the International Monetary Market of the Chicago Mercantile Exchange. Swiss banks, too, will store gold for you. There are also safe deposit companies that operate independently of banks.

20. *If I am going to speculate in gold, what is my most important tool?*

Gold is traded 18 hours a day, in various markets around the world. You must deal with a brokerage firm that provides trading facilities in London and Hong Kong, as well as New York and Chicago. In this manner you are not bound to U.S. trading hours. You can buy or sell gold 18 hours a day. You have a safe entrance or exit while your competitors sleep.

Chapter 13

A Monetary and Foreign Exchange Glossary of Terms

"A gold price adjustment should be looked upon not as a sin, but as a contribution to the achievement of such basic objectives as sustainable economic growth and reasonable freedom in trade and payments."

—*Dr. Miroslav A. Kriz*

Actual—The physical commodity (e.g., gold) as opposed to futures contracts.

ADR—American Depository Receipt issued by an American bank. The bank first buys a security in a foreign company, then issues an ADR to represent the security. Thus, whoever buys the ADR has the ultimate claim on the underlying stock. The purpose of issuing ADRs is to simplify the physical handling of securities of foreign issuers, which sometimes can be cumbersome.

Arbitrage—Buying of foreign exchange, securities, or commodities in one market and simultaneously selling in another market. By this technique a profit can be made because of differences in rates of exchange or in prices of securities or commodities.

Balance of Payments—Net difference of all credits and debits from one country to another.

Barter—Exchange of commodities, using value of merchandise as compensation instead of money. This method has been employed in recent years by countries in which currencies are blocked.

Big Three—The term used to refer to the three biggest banks in Switzerland. They are Swiss Bank Corporation, Union Bank of Switzerland, and Swiss Credit Bank.

Big Five—A term used in British banking referring to the five largest commercial banks in Great Britain. These are Midland Bank, Ltd.; Barclay's Bank, Ltd.; National Provincial Bank, Ltd.; Lloyd's Bank, Ltd.; and Westminster Bank, Ltd.

Bullion—Gold in bars or ingots, assaying at least .995 fine.

Central Bank—An agency that has been set up by the government of a country to supervise generally its banking system and its currency, and to act as its alter ego in financial matters.

Commodity—Generally speaking, any raw material, whether it is a mining product or of agricultural origin. A long list of commodities may be traded by the investor, either through leading stock brokerage firms that also trade commodities, or through firms that specialize in commodities. Each commodity exchange usually has specific trading units—that is, minimum quantities of a particular commodity that you can trade.

Conversion—Actual exchange of currency of one country for that of another. Such transactions usually pass through banking channels.

Convertibility—Ability of any holder of a currency to exchange it at will and on demand into any other currency or into gold.

Debasement—In modern terminology the reduction in the purchasing power or value of a currency in circulation as the result of constantly increasing prices. Earlier the term referred to a reduction in the precious metal content of gold and silver coins in favor of a greater proportion of lead, zinc, or other non-precious metals.

Devaluation—Lowering the exchange value of a currency, in terms of others, for any reason, such as external overvaluation. For gold standard currencies, devaluation is effected by first raising the price of gold in terms of the currency. This automatically decreases the number of units of other gold standard currencies required to purchase a given number of units of the first currency. Basic reasons for devaluation are usually overspending by a government.

Dirty Float—A situation that occurs when a government intervenes in the foreign exchange market while usually claiming that it isn't intervening.

Discount—A rate of exchange lower than spot, the spot rate expressed in terms of percentage per annum or points on which a dealer buys or sells foreign exchange for forward delivery.

Eurodollars—U.S. dollars held on deposit with banks outside the United States and used by them to meet their own temporary needs for additional liquidity or to extend loans to commercial borrowers. Loosely, any dollars held by anyone anywhere outside the United States.

Fineness—The purity of gold or silver as a percentage of the total gross weight. Thus, when one says that gold is .995 fine, it is meant that 99.5 percent of the weight is pure gold.

Floating—When central banks do not protect either upper or lower currency fluctuation limits a currency is said to be floating.

Foreign Exchange—A general term applied to transactions between countries or private citizens involving purchases and sales of foreign (other than local) currencies.

Forward Transaction—A transaction in currency whose value date is longer than two days after trade date (one day for Canada and Mexico).

Future Exchange Contract—A contract, usually between a bank and its customers, for the purchase or sale of foreign exchange at a fixed rate, with delivery at a specified time. It is generally used when customers want to preclude risks of fluctuations in rates of foreign exchange on funds due them at a future time.

"Gnomes of Zurich"—Figure of speech, often applied humorously to custodians of numbered banking accounts and to foreign exchange dealers in banking houses along the Bahnhofstrasse in Zurich, Switzerland. The phrase is attributed to George Brown, deputy prime minister of Great Britain in 1964, who blamed defects of the English pound on the "gnomes of Zurich."

Hedge—Purchase or sale of foreign exchange to protect an asset or liability. This action ensures a fixed dollar rate for conversion of foreign currency.

IMF—The abbreviation for International Monetary Fund, the organization set up at the Bretton Woods, New Hampshire, conference in 1944. The IMF has about 111 members whose duty it is to register their rates of exchange in terms of American dollars and maintain the rates. It was the IMF that began issuing so-called Special Drawing Rights or SDRs back in the 1960s. The SDRs, or "paper gold," were used to settle accounts between countries on the same basis as gold.

Inconvertibility—This is the converse of convertibility and implies simply that any holder of a currency which is inconvertible has no statutory right to demand conversion of that currency into any other currency or gold. Any such conversion is entirely at the discretion of authorities in the countries concerned. Usually conversion in these countries is exercised through some form of exchange control under which applications must be made to authorities for permits.

Inflation—It has been aptly said that a country suffers from inflation of its currency when there is too much money chasing too few goods. Money, by itself, is useless. Its utility lies only in its ability to act as a medium of exchange and purchasing agent. Government budgets that produce excesses of national spending over income (called "deficit financing") are prime inflators of internal currency and credit systems. Inflation actually takes place when more purchasing power (from credits raised by a government) is put into the hands of a community than is withdrawn via taxation. When increases in money supply or spending power are not offset by increases in productivity, resulting in more goods on sale against increases in money supplies, those in possession of excess spending power will use it, paying higher prices for limited amounts of goods offered for sale. This touches off a general rise in price levels, inevitably causing demand for higher wages, and another swirl in a vicious inflationary spiral.

Lot—The basic trading unit in gold coins. For example, a lot contains twenty Mexican 50-peso pieces or twenty U.S. double eagles.

Par of Exchange—An equivalent of a unit of money in one country expressed in the currency of another, using gold as a standard of value (par value).

Premium (in foreign exchange)—Rate of exchange, higher than spot rate, expressed in percentage per annum or points, on which a dealer buys or sells foreign exchange for forward delivery.

Premium (in coins)—The difference between a coin's market value and the value of the metallic content of the coin.

Price Limit—The maximum price move allowed by exchange rules for a given commodity for any one day's trading.

Rate of Exchange—An expression signifying a basis upon which the money of one country will be exchanged for that of another.

Realized Exchange Gain or Loss—A gain or loss resulting from conversion of one currency into another. It often applies to a gain or loss of subsidiary companies abroad, arising from settled or unsettled transactions in foreign currencies, particularly when unsettled balances are in a current working capital position.

Recession—A period of two consecutive calendar quarters when GNP (Gross National Product, the total of all goods and services produced in a nation) declines in terms of 1958 dollars.

Reserve Currency—One currency widely accepted by many nations' central banks in exchange for local currencies. There must be enough confidence in a reserve currency to result in a willingness by these nations to exchange. Until recently the U.S. dollar was an effective world reserve currency.

Revaluation—A somewhat ambiguous term that can mean either a retraction from too great a devaluation of a currency or the adjustment of a condition in which a currency has been undervalued externally.

SDR (Special Drawing Right)—A means by which existing international reserve assets may be supplemented periodically through a process of international decision, at rates relative to the world's needs.

Security Deposit—A cash amount that must be deposited with the broker for each contract as a guarantee of fulfillment of the futures contract. It is not considered as part payment of purchase. Some exchanges call this margin.

Short—The market position of a futures contract seller whose sale obligates him to deliver the commodity unless he liquidates his contract by an offsetting purchase; also the holder of a short position in the market.

Spread—A market position that is simultaneously long and short equivalent amounts of the same or related commodities. In some markets the term "straddle" is used synonymously.

Straddle—Also known as a "spread," the purchase of one future month against the sale of another future month of the same commodity. A straddle trade is based on a price relationship between the two months and a belief that the "spread," or difference in price between the two contract months, will change sufficiently to make the trade profitable.

Swap—A simultaneous purchase and sale (or sale and purchase) of a foreign currency, mostly against U.S. dollars. This transaction does not protect against risk of parity change. Swaps are a method of funding foreign currency borrowings through a secondary currency.

Troy Ounce—A system of weights in which twelve troy ounces make a pound; gold and silver are measured in troy ounces, which is the system widely used by jewelers in the United States and England.

NOTE
For a more comprehensive glossary we recommend *Financial Tactics & Terms for the Sophisticated International Investor,* by Dr. Harry Schultz, Harper & Row, $7.95, 176 pages.

Appendix

Where You Can Get Help

There are a number of organizations devoted to gold and gold related services. The following list is not exhaustive by any means, but will get you started.

Bullion and Coin Dealers

J. Aron & Co. Inc.
160 Water Street
New York, New York 10038

Deak-Perera
630 Fifth Avenue
New York, New York 10020

Engelhard Minerals & Chemicals Corporation
430 Mountain Avenue
Murray Hill, New Jersey 07974

Mocatta Metals Corporation
25 Broad Street
New York, New York 10004

James Sinclair Commodities
90 Broad Street
New York, New York 10004

Brokerage Firms With A Special Interest In Gold, Gold
Futures and Gold Shares

Drexel Burnham Lambert
60 Broad Street
New York, New York 10004

Merrill Lynch, Pierce, Fenner & Smith Inc.
1 Liberty Plaza
165 Broadway
New York, New York 10006

James Sinclair & Company
90 Broad Street
New York, New York 10004

Investment Letters Giving Advice on Gold Vehicles

International Harry Schultz Letter
P.O. Box 134
Princeton, New Jersey 08540

Gold Newsletter published by
National Committee for Monetary Reform
1524 Hillary Street
New Orleans, Louisiana 70118

International Investor Viewpoint
610 S.W. Alder Street
Portland, Oregon 97205

The Numisco Letter
175 W. Jackson Blvd.
Ste A-640
Chicago, Illinois 60604

James Sinclair Investment Advisory Service
90 Broad Street
New York, New York 10004

Index